The Parish
Development
Process

The Parish
Development
Process

Marvin T. Judy

Abingdon Press
Nashville   New York

THE PARISH DEVELOPMENT PROCESS

Copyright © 1973 by Abingdon Press

This volume is an enlargement and revision of *The Cooperative Parish in Nonmetropolitan Areas*, copyright © 1967 by Abingdon Press. That volume was based on *The Larger Parish and Group Ministry*, copyright © 1959 by Abingdon Press, which was enlarged from *Serve to Survive*, copyright © 1957 by Marvin T. Judy and assigned to Abingdon Press. The pamphlet *Parish Development Aids*, published by Abingdon Press in 1964, has also been incorporated into this volume.

Library of Congress Cataloging in Publication Data

JUDY, MARVIN T. The parish development process. "An enlargement and revision of The cooperative parish in nonmetropolitan areas."

Bibliography: p.
1. Larger parishes. I. Title.
BV638.4.J792   254   72-8819

ISBN 0-687-30086-X

MANUFACTURED BY THE PARTHENON PRESS AT
NASHVILLE, TENNESSEE, UNITED STATES OF AMERICA

To
Murlene Oleta Judy
Companion, Counselor, Collaborator

Preface

The first basic thesis presented in this book, which is applicable in any segment of culture whether rural or urban, is: *Where a change has taken place in population, racial, ethnic, or socio-economic levels, and there are existing churches, the cooperative parish may offer the structure for an effective ministry.* The form of ministry needs to be determined by the laity of the churches involved, and their decision needs to be based upon thorough investigation of existing conditions both within the congregations and in the area in which the churches are located. Sound research based upon sociological methods assists in gaining the necessary information for decision and an understanding of alternate plans for organization.

A second thesis of the book is: *Organizational structure and the employed professional church staff are to assist the laity to be the church in worship, nurture, and at work in the world.* This, I feel, is sound theology of the organized church consisting of laymen and ministers. With these two basic theses the book is designed to assist one or more congregations of one or more denominations within a given geographic area—rural or urban—to design a structure for an effective witness of the church in worship, in nurture or learning, and at work in the world.

The book has developed out of previous writings, additional research, and many experiences across the nation in short-term schools on parish development. I am indebted to hundreds of people who have tested ideas and have helped to refine the process of parish development.

The first writing of background material for this book was in 1957 when I was invited to participate in a three-weeks' school at Candler School of Theology, Emory University. Thirty persons were carefully selected to screen a manuscript I had written entitled *Serve to Survive*. The basic idea within the book was taken from the teachings of Jesus: If one is to save one's life, one must lose it. The cooperative parish is a serving institution first. In serving the saving factor enters in. After a thorough analysis of the manuscript the book was rewritten and was published by Abingdon Press in 1959 under the title, *The Larger Parish and Group Ministry*. In 1964 Abingdon Press published my thirty-five page pamphlet entitled *Parish Development Aids*. *The Larger Parish and Group Ministry* was used as the basic text by a group of people in a local area for a study in determining their organizational needs. By 1966 the supply of the basic text was exhausted, and it was felt the book needed to be revised. The new and enlarged book, entitled *The Cooperative Parish in Nonmetropolitan Areas*, was published by Abingdon Press in 1967. This book also incorporated the 1964 pamphlet.

I am indebted to many people for their help in formulating ideas. The most helpful has been my wife, Murlene Judy, who has shared with me eighteen years of pastoral ministries in both rural and urban areas, has participated in many seminars on parish development across the nation, and has constantly read, digested, and assimilated literature for our use as our ministry has continued in seminary teaching. Without this latter contribution I could never keep up with the massive amount of literature being produced. She has been a sounding board for my ideas and a producer of many creative and innovative concepts of ministry.

A word of thanks is also expressed to our daughter-in-law, Sharon Judy, for her patience in assisting to prepare the typescript for the book.

The book is presented in the hope that it can be an instrument for perfecting the work of congregations and ministers in meeting the religious needs of a people within a given area and in the world.

MARVIN T. JUDY

Contents

CONTENTS

I

Why the Cooperative Parish

Beginnings

Various forms of the cooperative parish have been in operation since the beginning of the Christian church. The house congregation was part of a unit ministered to by one pastor as he moved from group to group. The deacon in the third century became an out-of-the-church pastor visiting the sick, the prisoner, and the other persons who could not meet with the assembled congregation. The mission church sponsored by a congregation has been a usual form of the spreading of the gospel. The circuit system whereby congregations shared their pastor has been a standard practice of all denominations including the Roman Catholic, though the term was popularized by the early Methodists in both England and America.

The cooperative parish as a planned organization of cooperating congregations in this century is usually attributed to Harlow S. Mills. Mills, following the sudden death of his wife, was faced with the tempting offer by his denomination (Congregational) to become an executive of a state board and the offer of an assistantship in a large urban church. He attempted to work through the meaning of his own ministry and to discover where his ministry could best be filled. He had been pastor of the Congregational church in Benzonia, Michigan, for fifteen years. His feelings are recorded in his own work *The Making of a Country Parish.*

> For fifteen years I had been working away in my country parish. They had been happy years of glad, harmonious work. I was satisfied with my job. Though remote from the great centers of population, in a small village, and with people of very modest means, that restless feeling that spoils the preacher and mars the work of so many ministers had been absent. My people were of the strong and sturdy sort, faithful and appreciative beyond many, ready to cooperate in carrying out any plan of work that the pastor might purpose. . . .
>
> I spent some weeks and months in considering these propositions and finally turned them down. I could not bring myself to sever my connections with those to whom I had been so long and so closely related. The personal tie was too strong and I decided to remain with my people.[1]

Mills then began to visualize what the possibility might be for expanding the work of his ministry.

> The vision expanded until it took in another township, and parts of three of four more. It became plain that almost half a county was tributary to the church, that five hundred families and twenty-five hundred people were waiting my ministry.
>
> It dawned upon my mental vision that I was called upon to be the pastor of all these people, for five or six miles in every direction, that the Benzonia church was responsible for them all, that they had a right to look to us for service

and help, and if we failed to give it we should be unfaithful to our Master and recreant to our trust. Then I said: "Here is something worth doing. Here may be wrought out an experiment in country evangelization and rural betterment that may help to arrest the downward trend that has become so alarming in these latter days . . .

And then came the vision of "The Larger Parish." I saw the church reaching out its hand and touching tenderly but effectively all the people in the surrounding country. I saw the church feeling some responsibility for every family, and counting them all as within the bounds of the parish. I saw every family in all that wide region as tributary to the church. I saw the church making systematic plans to carry the gospel to all these outlying neighborhoods. I began to think of all those people as my parishoners as truly as were those who lived near the church and were members of it. And so the vision dawned upon me of the Larger Parish.[2]

A house-to-house visitation was made by Mills in the next few months for a distance of six to eight miles in every direction from the church. New preaching places were established. Additional ministerial leadership was employed, and a staff ministry came into being.

Mills later formulated his basic philosophy for the larger parish under five convictions: (1) The real object of the church is to serve people, and its claim for support should rest upon the same ground upon which every other institution bases its claim for support—that it gives value received; (2) the church must serve *all* people within a given geographic area; (3) the church must serve *all* the interests of the people; (4) the village church, if it would fulfill its mission, must be responsible for the country evangelization; (5) if the village church would fulfill its mission, it must be a community church.[3]

These visions were the motivational force behind Mills work. Though they occurred more than a half century ago

they are contemporary with modern needs. It was moti-
vated out of a deep compassion for persons. It came from a
dedicated life realizing there was a framework of organization which could serve as a means for a meaningful and
fruitful ministry. This ministry was to be to persons individually and corporately—personal and social—all needs
of all people being met by all congregations within the
trade area community. By *all needs* Mills meant economic,
educational, health, welfare, political, recreational, conservation as well as religious. By *all persons* Mills meant
people within the churches and people out of the church,
persons of all social and economic levels, and persons of all
racial and ethnic backgrounds. Here was a combination
of the personal and social gospel in action.

Like Mills in rural Michigan, a young seminarian in
New York had a vision of ministry to the socially, ec-
onomically, and racially disinherited. Don Benedict had
known of the price one pays for convictions as he had been
in prison as a conscientious objector to war. He later
changed his beliefs and was released from prison in 1943
to serve in the Second World War. In the fall of 1947 in
his senior year at Union Theological Seminary in New
York, Don was deeply impressed with the words in the
central window of the chapel, "Go ye into all the world,
and preach the gospel to every creature." "All the world"
for Benedict soon came to include East Harlem, "the hell
of Manhattan," a section of the city filled with hopeless,
frustrated humanity. He was joined by a fellow student
Bill Webber in making a study of the area. On foot they
walked through East Harlem. Their first descriptive notes
record:

Six-story cold-water tenements with moldering fire escapes.
Garbage everywhere: ashcans filled to overflowing: fires

18

burning in the gutter and on vacant lots. Broken glass on the street. Radios blaring. Small boys rushing out in front of speeding cars. Sidewalks teeming-Negroes, Puerto Ricans, Italians, Jews. A bleak empty space where a house had been torn down, leaving bricks and a grotesque iron bedstead, rusted and projecting out of the rubble. Small children in flimsy clothes play gaily among the debris; their bright smiles are a constrast to their elder brother's cynical attitude. No wonder.[4]

It was soon discovered by Benedict and Webber that East Harlem had a population of four thousand persons in one city block, packed into twenty seven rotting tenement apartments. There were two hundred thousand persons living in one square mile. It was known for its high rate of TB, VD, infant mortality, rat bites, malnutrition, crime, and dope.

They were joined by a Negro, Archie Hargroves, originally from North Carolina, who had known the problems of poverty and hunger. By sheer determination Hargroves had worked his way through college and seminary, and was now a Baptist minister determined to make the gospel come alive among the people in East Harlem where he had once lived.

The fame of the East Harlem Protestant Parish is now worldwide. Through original support by the Federal Council of Churches it got under way. Many denominations have supported the work, and it remains at this writing the most prominent inner city parish in America.

The parish was born out of a deep conviction that the leaders had to live out the gospel among these depressed people. It meant *identification,* and identification meant taking their families into the tenement house:

It would mean taking their families along, and exposing their children to the same temptations as the children who

19

lived next door. It would mean being always at the disposal of the people with whom they sought identity, always having an open door, always responding to a visitor's knock, however late in the night it might come; it would mean, in other words, an abandonment of privacy and a free welcome into their family circle for the addicts and the drunks and the friendless and the thieves. Identification with East Harlem would mean looking down the dismal streets and saying, "This is my home; this is where I belong. . . ."

"But you'll never last here," a young man told Don Benedict. "Anyone who wasn't born here couldn't learn to stand it."

"You may be right," came the thoughtful answer. "You may very well be right." [5]

The young ministers early came to the realization that strict personal and group disciplines were necessary to sustain them in their mission. They constituted themselves into a group ministry in which they realized their strength was in the mutual support for one another. They adopted four disciplines:

1. *The devotional discipline.* Daily Bible-reading using the same scripture was to be the center of their discipline. Once a week they would meet to study the scripture and to receive the Sacrament of Holy Communion. Out of each six months they would spend three days in retreat for spiritual renewal. There would be a visible center for worship in each home.

2. *The economic discipline.* Salaries would be on the basis of actual need. There would be a common fund from honoraria received by any member of the group and dispersed for emergency needs.

3. *Vocational discipline.* This consisted of a covenant to devote their ministry in the slums. Monthly plans were to be exposed to one another for criticism and coordina-

tion. Vocational change would be made only in consultation with one another.

4. *The political discipline.* Appropriate legislation concerning East Harlem was to be hammered out and worked for. If one in the group could not conscientiously support some legislation, he would keep silent.

It may be observed that in both the Benzonia Larger Parish and the East Harlem Protestant Parish there were fundamental principles which were the same. Some of these are enumerated: (1) A deep concern for the needs of people both religious and personal. (2) A deep concern for changing the social and economic environment in which persons were forced to live. (3) A deep conviction that the ministry was too large for one minister to perform and was too large for one congregation. It demanded group ministry of ministers and churches. (4) The task required self-identification of each leader with the people he would be serving and a strong self-discipline in vocation, personal growth, and corporate support. (5) Though denominationally supported, the denomination took a secondary position in favor of service to persons.

In addition to the principles derived from the above descriptions, there are a number of basic principles in regard to motivation for cooperative parishes and practical frameworks for efficient parish management.

Basic Thesis for Cooperative Parish

A basic thesis for cooperative parishes is: Where a change has taken place in population, racial, ethnic, or socio-economic levels, and there are existing churches, the cooperative parish may offer the structure for an effective ministry.

Population shifts are inevitable and are always taking place. When a shift reaches a stage where the normal

21

transactions of life are seriously interrupted, then new forms of ministry are called for. In the United States there has been a constant decrease of population in approximately one-half of the counties. Between 1960 and 1970, 53 percent, or 1612, of the nation's 3,042 counties lost population. The trend is that counties that lost population in the 1960s were generally the ones that had been losing population during the 1940-60 period. The majority of the counties that are showing declining population are in the southern and north central states. Some 1300 of the 1612 counties losing population are in a broad loop of states running from the Dakotas and Minnesota, south to Texas, and east to Georgia and the Carolinas and the Appalachian region of West Virginia, Kentucky, and Tennessee. This has been the result of the agricultural revolution and technology moving from a human-and animal-powered agriculture to a machine-powered operation. At the same time the industrial revolution primarily centered in major cities has provided a vast labor market. This has been like a giant magnet drawing persons from rural areas to urban. Thousands of small towns have become smaller, and other thousands of rural neighborhoods have less than half the population they had at the beginning of this century. Such shifts in population have left once-thriving congregations with a smaller number of participants and with church buildings, which once knew of two to three hundred active members, housing a congregation of fifty. It is disheartening to conduct a service of worship with thirty persons in a building which will seat two hundred.

The shift within the city of persons from older, many times elite areas, to the fringe of the city and the suburbs, has meant a new population moving in. Multiple housing in what was once a single-family, mansion-type home, conversion of residental areas to part business and industry, the building of low income apartments has changed the social, economic, and many times, the racial and ethnic characteristics of thousands of cities. In the midst of such change stands majestic "old First Church" or "Grace Church" or "St. Johns." These usually are large structures well built, but housing a dying congregation. The real problem is how to minister to the new population now surrounding the church? Not only do the people near the church building need spiritual nurture in worship and Christian education as the original residents of the neighborhood did, but they need jobs, medical care, food, and, above all, a sense of personhood.

The 1970 census of population reveal the nation's 230 Standard Metropolitan Statistical Areas had 85 percent of the nation's population increase between 1960 and 1970. A Standard Metropolitan Statistical Area (SMSA) is a region in which there is one city of fifty thousand population or more, or contiguous cities with a total of fifty thousand, and includes the basic area around the city or cities where the economic and communications patterns are dominated by the population centers or central city. The SMSA is composed of one or several counties, and all population within the area is considered urban. Nonmetropolitan areas refers to that part of the nation's population which is outside of one of the 230 SMSAs. The increase in metropolitan areas was 15.1 percent and nonmetropolitan areas was 5.1 percent. A closer look, however, reveals a definite city-suburb disparity. While central cities (the city or cities at the center of an SMSA) increased by 4.7 percent, the suburban rings around cities increased 25.6 percent. The nation's SMSAs now have more suburban dwellers than city dwellers. In fact there are now more people living in suburbs than either the central cities or the nonmetropolitan areas of the nation. Population in the suburban rings stands at 74 million, with 62 million in the central cities and 64 million outside the SMSAs. Central cities and suburban rings were equal in 1960 with 59 million, a shift from 1950 when city population stood 13 million higher than the suburban rings.

Central cities in the larger metropolitan areas actually lost population during the 1960s by 700,000 or 3.1 percent. Of the fourteen central cities with 2 million or more in the SMSA, only Los Angeles gained.

Nonmetropolitan growth in the 1960s was greater in the Northwest and West. The South with 44.3 percent of its residents outside metropolitan areas, remains the most rural section of the nation. In the West, only 22.4 percent, and in the Northwest, only 20.4 percent of the people live outside the city-suburb complexes.

Some effects of population shifts upon the church are (1) the "orphaned" congregation in rural areas. This is a church which was once strong. It may have been a part of a pastoral charge which now has disintegrated. The church is left alone, too weak to supply an adequate ministry and program. (2) A group of congregations of one or several denominations in town and country areas which need to band together to provide an adequate ministry. (3) The need to supply a ministry in rapidly growing suburbia where it is difficult to start a congregation, erect a church structure, and maintain a ministry and program. (4) The need to provide a ministry in an area of rapid transition within the city. Old existing congregations are frustrated with the changing population surrounding the church and feel inadequate in ministry. They need the strength of other cooperating congregations to continue this service to the area in which they are located. (5) The inner city, or that part of the city which has experienced the most radical change, is in need of highly specialized ministries to meet the needs of cultural and racial groups, poverty, disease, crime, and delinquency. The oldest congregations of the city are located there, but, in many cases, they are almost totally inadequate, alone, to cope with the needs. Interchurch cooperation is essential to provide an economic base for adequate leadership and program.

A Wise Use of Ministerial Resources

The cooperative parish in one of its forms provides the structure for a more efficient, challenging, and satisfying use of ministerial resources in both rural and urban areas.

One of the major problems facing most Protestant denominations is the need for a more efficient use of ministerial resources. An illustration of this is that in The United Methodist Church 51 percent of the ministers are serving three hundred members or less. Dissatisfaction comes in the ministry when a task is too small to be challenging. It has been found in the field of personnel management that when persons are consulted about their work, most feel they do not have enough work rather than too much. The seminarian finishes the seven-year college and seminary career and accepts his first call or assignment only to find, in many cases, his pastoral responsibility is far below his capabilities. The cooperative parish provides the structure to strengthen the pastoral load.

The cooperative parish provides the structure for use of specialized church workers. Some denominations have persons who are especially trained in church and community ministries, or there are persons who have training in the fields of music, education, youth work, social service, nursing, or recreation. Special talents, abilities, or training can be utilized quite effectively in the cooperative parish either on a full-time or part-time basis.

The lay ministry can be utilized effectively in the cooperative parish. Many persons feel a call to the ministry but for some reason have not been able to prepare themselves academically for full ordination within their denomination. There is an increasing number of persons who are wanting to devote post-retirement years to the ministry. With retirement becoming possible at a relatively younger age, the supply of such persons is getting larger. Their talents need to be utilized by the church. This can be done efficiently and effectively in cooperation with fully trained and ordained clergy in a cooperative parish.

A Full Ministry for All Persons

Within the Christian tradition the believer expresses his faith in personal development and in service. This takes the form of worship, education, evangelism, mission, social concerns, and stewardship. The church needs to provide full opportunity for such expressions. This is difficult in a small, isolated congregation, or with inadequate ministerial leadership or housing and equipment.

With several congregations pooling their resources within a given geographic area it becomes possible to provide a broader base for a fuller participation of each person within the area in the Christian enterprise.

As with Harlow Mills in Benzonia, Michigan, and Don Benedict and Bill Webber in East Harlem, New York, the cooperative parish provides a structure for the careful examination of all the needs of all the people within the area. Too often a single congregation is quite satisfied to provide a partial ministry for its member families only. A just criticism of the church has been its lack of concern for the physical, educational, social, economic, and humanitarian needs of the people who live in the vicinity of the

26

church. Examining the materials in this book, one will see how such needs can be discovered and how the cooperative parish may provide the structure to meet the needs.

Cooperation with Private and Governmental Agencies

There are an increasing number of agencies within every community both rural and urban that are attempting to meet human needs. The work of such agencies is often handicapped because of an inability of the leaders to reach the persons most in need. The church with its traditional benevolent work may be the catalyst to bring together agencies and needy people. The impact of a group of churches of the same or different denominations provides leadership, building facilities, and a ready resource for agencies to make more effective their work. The debate at this point is not over how involved the local church should be in social action or how many government agencies there should be, but how well the needs of people are being met. Is proverty being eliminated, are persons gaining an education, are the social and recreational opportunities conducive to personal growth and a healthy maturing of children, youth, and adults, are the problems of health being met, is crime diminishing, is there being developed a better relationship between racial and ethnic groups? A local congregation needs to be examining each of the areas mentioned, but a group of congregations can pool their resources and do a far more adequate job of ministry and of assisting agencies in their tasks.

The Interdenominational Possiblities

The twentieth century has been a time of church union for some of the major denominations, or branches of de-

27

nominations. At the same time it has been the scene for the birth of numerous sects and cults. The most outstanding movement has been the Council on Church Union (CO CU), which proposes to bring under one administrative pattern nine of the major Protestant denominations. At this writing the enthusiasm for COCU has cooled. Laymen and many ministers are saying it is not union we want but interchurch cooperation. We have reached a common theological understanding on many of the basic tenets of the Christian faith, but church polity and government are so deeply rooted that it will be many years before ministers and laymen can overcome in actual union the sense of being personally threatened. Nonetheless there is an urgent need for cooperation between churches of the same denomination and of different denominations. The cooperative parish in its varied forms provides the structural framework for interdenominational cooperation. This can be on a very tenuous or intense basis. It may be a joint project within the area, or it may be a structured ministry in many areas including worship, education, and social action. Experience has shown that when congregations begin working together, the dynamic of human relations will develop to where persons come to know and trust one another, and denominational prejudices tend to diminish.

The Theological Imperative

A basic thesis concerning the church can be repeated: The professional ministry and the employed staff and organizational structures are for the purpose of assisting the laity to be the church in worship, nurture, and at work in the world.[6]

The church is the body of believers, both clergy and laity. The real dynamic of the church rests in the covenant people, the people of God, as they develop a sustaining relationship within the body through worship, nurture, and fellowship and become the dynamic church at work in the world. The world includes the area of the local congregation as well as the mission of the church in distant lands.

The covenant community is brought into being through the unmerited grace and love of God. Persons are saved by grace. Salvation is *now*. It brings to the individual the wholeness of life. It gives a focus for existence and meaning for life in the world. The church is the corporate body, composed of those who have known God's grace. This community of believers, or the people of God, is created in order that the mercy and grace known and experienced may be shared with all mankind. It is not an end in itself, but a means to the sharing of the Good News with others.

The structure is the means of communicating the basic theology of the church. Christianity began as the servant community. Jesus said of himself, "I am among you as one who serves"; "The servant is not greater than his master"; "He that will be greatest among you, let him be a servant." Again Jesus exhorted, "He that will lose his life will find it." It is the servant community which will survive in the world.

The theological imperative for the cooperative parish lies at the point where people of God in different congregations within a given geographic area find a means of ministry to all the people and all the needs of the people within the area. We can do no other and remain true to the Christian imperative.[7]

II

Meaningful Locality Groups in Nonmetropolitan Areas

A locality group as used in this writing may be defined as follows: a segment of society which has enough cultural characteristics such as socio-economic levels, housing patterns, land-use designs, work-travel movements, trade-travel movements, natural or man-made barriers, that it may be distinguished from another cultural group.

In considering any type of cooperative parish, the locality group is of paramount importance. Cooperation between congregations will be in direct proportion to the intensity of human contacts made in everyday work, trade, and associational relationships. A tightly organized cooperative parish, for instance, which requires frequent contacts of persons involved and a rather rigid organizational structure, should be confined to a small locality group in either a rural or urban setting. More loosely cooperative parish structures can be spread to a larger, less integrated locality group. More will be said in this relationship at the end of the chapter and in chapter 4 on parish structures.

Locality Group I: The Rural Neighborhood

Land settlement in pioneer America was primarily that of the rural neighborhood. As pioneers established their residence on the land it was in clusters of farmsteads. The distance across a neighborhood was that which could be traveled by horseback, buggy, wagon, or on foot. In practice, this turned out to be about three miles from the neighborhood center, or six miles both ways. Settlement followed a definite pattern. First was built the house for residence. Second, a group of neighbors built a school. Third, someone would establish a small business, usually a general merchandise store; and fourth, they built a church. The persons living in the service area of the church and school were dependent upon one another for fellowship and social life, mutual aid in times of disaster and sickness, and mutual exchange of tools and work. The neighborhood was named and took on recognizable characteristics. It played a vital role in the life of the nation. It was the center of elementary school activities. In it was the church—one or more congregations. In the neighborhood were to be found a general merchandise store, a blacksmith shop, and sometimes a medical doctor. The neighborhood was isolated due to poor roads and slow transporation. It was necessary for a church and school to be established within the neighborhood structure if the people of the area were to have educational and religious opportunities. A neighborhood was compelled to be self-sufficient in most respects. Only the merchant made his way, with any degree of regularity, out of the neighborhood for the purpose of replenishing his supply of goods.

In the intimacy of the neighborhood, children were born, reared, educated, nurtured in religious living, married, and found their place in the economy of the area and

31

conformed to the mores of the group. The cemetery became a part of the neighborhood structure usually close to the one-room church.

Such neighborhoods, three to six miles in diameter, have become the romantic symbol of rural America. The little red schoolhouse has been the place where many of our American statesmen and leaders found their early training. Stories and novels have been written by the scores about romantic pioneer American.

The rural neighborhood has been the subject of many studies by rural sociologists. Entire texts have been devoted to the study of rural society with primary emphasis upon the rural neighborhood. Among the many definitions the most common is: "A rural neighborhood consists of an area in which people neighbor together; that is, visit, borrow tools and equipment, trade, work, and cooperate in various ways." [1] The rural neighborhood is usually composed of ten to twenty families living close enough to visit one another, developing a common bond of friendship. There may be one or more institutions in the rural neighborhood. This can be a church, elementary school, general store, or a combination of these. There may be no institutions, but merely a social unit built around fellowship of common interests.

The rural neighborhood is rapidly changing. Good roads, modern automobiles and trucks have made the agricultural town, or even the distant city, very close to the residents of the rural neighborhood. The general merchandise store has dwindled in business until no longer does it have an adequate trade to warrant operation. Thousands of such crossroads stores have ceased to be. It takes less time for the rural neighborhood family to drive five to fifteen miles to town than it did for their grandparents to go three miles for their trading.

The one-room country school all across America is rapidly becoming a memory. Good roads and the school bus have brought consolidation, forcing the children to go to the larger school in town or a new consolidated school in a different neighborhood. Through state control of funds, consolidation has been forced upon many rural neighborhoods whether the people wanted it or not. General opinion, however, at this time, is that consolidation is worth what it costs in neighborhood morale because of the compensation of a much better quality of education.

Neighborhood rural churches by the thousands have suffered a like fate as that of the stores and schools. It has been estimated that the Protestant churches of America have been closing two thousand rural churches a year since 1930. There is no question that many of these churches have served their period of usefulness, for they have been the source of Christian guidance through the decades. The primary difficulty has been the lack of any systematic procedure devised by denominational executives for the closing of a rural church. The usual pattern has been that the church continued to weaken until the few remaining members became so discouraged that they finally, with a sigh, just let the program of the church go.

Sometimes the closing of a rural church has led to the reviving of a village church. The leaders in the rural church move their membership to a town or village church. However, the larger group of people in the rural church have not aligned themselves with another church, and thus they are lost to the membership of the church and left without a church home. This pattern calls for some systematic method of neighborhood study to be made before a church closes or is consolidated with another church.

In spite of the thousands of rural neighborhood churches which have closed in recent years, there are still thousands

33

of them in existence. In The United Methodist Church alone, there are approximately fifteen thousand rural neighborhood churches.

Many studies have revealed that at this writing there are within the nation—with the exception of mountain regions, deserts, or heavily wooded areas—a rural church on the average of every three to four miles, and a church of the same denomination every six to seven miles.

What is the future of the rural neighborhood? This is a question the rural sociologist is asking across America. In the early thirties the opinion prevailed that the rural neighborhood was rapidly ceasing to be. Such an attitude aided in public school consolidation. Nevertheless, in a few years the sociologist was saying that the rural neighborhood was persisting, it was going to remain, at least for a time, as a part of American culture. It was discovered that when the school went out of existence, when the church died, when the store was gone, informal groups sprang up. They were primarily for the purpose of fellowship and the desire of the individual for communication with friends of a like mind. In more recent years there has been a re-emphasis upon the vanishing rural neighborhood. Sociologists are not agreed. It is possible that the rural neighborhood is ceasing to function as an organizational unit but that it will remain as a social unit. Some sociologists believe that it is a part of the rural culture, the same as the family, and plays a vital role in cultural development.

It has been discovered through studies made over a number of years in the same areas, that there are approximately one-half of the meaningful rural neighborhoods in existence that were present fifty years ago. Where a neighborhood has existed there is usually one institution such as a school, church, store, cheese factory, creamery, cotton gin, or other form of economic institution.

Social contacts of various kinds play an important role in neighborhood solidarity, but they also tend to form new relationships which reach across neighborhood boundaries. Saddle clubs, hunting clubs, dance clubs, school activities stemming from a consolidated school make for associational groups which are not necessarily neighborhood-centered but interest-centered. This is also an urban trend as is reflected in urban associational patterns which have little connection with residential patterns.

It has also been discovered that through overt efforts on the part of outside leaders in farm organizations, churches, political or business agencies, the neighborhood could be retained as a meaningful group.

A factor of major importance in present cultural trends is the increasing outmigration of urban dwellers to the countryside. Modern transportation has made it possible for many people to have their country dwelling and their city work too. Also the second home in the country within a one-hundred-mile radius of major cities is changing the complexion of the neighborhood. The centers of recreation on lake and stream are attracting thousands of urban dwellers back to the country. Kolb describes an area near Madison, Wisconsin, where a rural church burned and was rebuilt to fit the developing pattern of neighborhood settlement. He states:

Within this locality there are small farm families, part-time farmers, large farms with gentleman farmers as owners who are also commercial and professional people in the city, their resident renters, gardeners, artisans, clerical workers, a commercial orchard grower, and a church bishop. Families from the city come regularly to church services and to such local events as the Sunday afternoon horse races. Here is something different in group arrangements. Even the archi-

35

tecture of the new church is an announced symbol of this difference, a transitional type of community relations, neither rural or urban, neither urban or suburban, not even metropolitan, but neopolitan, like the early commune, a new form for a very old kind of group association where nearly every element of population and variety of occupation in the general society is represented within the local community.[2]

There is an increasing body of literature emphasizing the importance of nature in personal and cultural development, and the primary group as the means of establishing and retaining value norms. The rural neighborhood has been a natural environment for family development, but with rapidly changing patterns of association it has the potential of disappearing in mass society. Architects are attempting to catch something of the beauty of nature in the greenery, living stream, and fountain in the midst of a sprawling shopping center. City planners are setting aside vast acreage for parks, and developers of new residential areas are attempting to preserve the natural beauty of trees, flowers, streams, and lakes. Nature is one thing, and the value of community life as has been associated with the rural neighborhood is another. However, persons in open country neighborhood churches can accept a new responsibility in the preservation of their church as a major factor in the expression of the gospel in the primary group relationship.

In the midst of such change stands the rural church. In spite of the thousands of these churches that have been closed, there are thousands of them still open. In some areas of America today 70 percent of the Protestant congregations are in open country. Most of these churches are small. Many of the churches must share a minister with another congregation to have a well-rounded program.

What will be the fate of the neighborhood church? The answer to this question depends upon the strategy of the Protestant church in town and country areas. Two general hypotheses can now be stated for serving people through the church in rural areas: (1) If the neighborhood church is needed as a unifying force in the rural neighborhood, the Christian community is duty bound to keep it there and provide an opportunity for a full program of church activity; (2) if the church is not needed as an institution within the neighborhood for a unifying force, then the people who reside there must be provided with ministerial leadership and a church in which they may express their religious devotion. This church will be in another neighborhood or community center. If the latter case is true, some means of drawing the people of the neighborhood together with people of the area in which the church is located must be discovered. It is possible that through a common trade center, consolidated schools, farm organizations, and church activities, the people will build natural affinities with one another. The major tragedy of the declining and dying neighborhood church has been that large groups of people have been left without a church tie of any kind. Neighborhood ties are so strong that there is no feeling of oneness with people of another neighborhood; yea, frequently feelings of animosity are felt between neighborhood groups preventing the affiliation with a church in another neighborhood.

Locality Group II: The Rural Community

The second cultural area in rural society is the rural community. The word "community" is being widely used by the theologian, philosopher, and sociologist. It is derived from the Latin *communis,* meaning "fellowship or community of relations or feelings." In medieval Latin it was used in the sense of a body of fellows or fellow townsmen. MacIver, in an early attempt at defining community, said, "By community I mean any area of common life, village, or town, or district, or county, or even wider area. To deserve the name community, the area must be somehow distinguished from another area, the common life may have some characteristics of its own such that the frontiers of the area have some meaning." [3] Kenvon L. Butterfield in 1918 distinguished the community from the neighborhood:

> I wish to emphasize one point strongly. We must not confuse "community" with "neighborhood." A neighborhood is simply a group of families living conveniently near together. The neighborhood can do a great many things, but it is not a community. A true community is a social group that is more or less self-sufficient. It is big enough to have its own center of interest—its trading center, its social center, its own church, its own school house, its own garage, its own library, and to possess such other institutions as the people of the community need. It is something more than a mere aggregation of families. There may be several neighborhoods in a community. A community is the smallest social unit that will hold together. . . . A community is a sort of individualized group of people. It is both the smallest and the largest number of people that can constitute a real social unit. It is a sort of family of familes. [4]

Butterfield would have his reader recognize a distinct difference between neighborhood and community. *This is important in our study for an understanding of the problems related to the rural church.* Sociologists have come to think of the rural community as consisting of a central town or village surrounded by several rural neighborhoods. In the central town will be found a sufficient number of institutions, as Butterfield so ably states above, to supply the day-by-day needs of the villager and resident of the rural neighborhoods. Dwight Sanderson in 1920 stated: "A rural community consists of the people in a local area tributary to the center of their common interests. The community is the smallest geographical unit of organized association of the chief human activities." [5] This definition has been the basis of many research projects, and along with the methods of community delineation has come what is probably the most universally accepted definition of rural community: "A rural community consists of the social interaction of people and their institutions in the local area in which they live on dispersed farm-steads and in a hamlet or village which forms the center of their common interests." [6] With Sanderson's insights as the basis of community definition, a working statement of the meaning of community is presented for the sake of analysis: (1) people and/or institutions in social interaction, (2) a definable geographical area, (3) a psychic feeling among individuals which gives a feeling of identity-with, (4) an understood relationship which controls the mores of the community life, (5) a constellation of institutions and services rendered for the benefit of the people of the community.

A brief discussion of each of the above is presented.

1. *People and/or institutions in social interaction.* Within the community structure there must be mutual sharing of time, energy, social activities, and institutional life. Every rural community has in it the opportunity for people to come in contact with one another. Families mix together in church, school, and business organizations, and are constantly having interaction either in cooperation or conflict. In short, people are thrown together in common

everyday activities. Individuals are known in those relations that naturally evolve out of such associations.

2. *A definable geographical area.* The territory for intimate social interaction is naturally limited by geography. There is a limit to which people can travel for trade, institutional, and social life. A later chapter will deal with methods of determining the geographical community boundary. This is a vitally important factor in church administrative areas.

3. *A psychic feeling among individuals which gives a feeling of identity-with.* The residents of a community quickly come to identify themselves with the community in which they reside. One can ask the question, "What is your community?" and an answer will be given, "Pleasant Valley" or "Centerville." There is a loyalty developed in the mind of the resident. This is expressed in civic pride, support of school athletic groups, church, and community enterprises.

4. *An understood relationship which controls the mores of the community life.* Every community has personality. Customs are established which carry over from generation to generation. Many times customs are difficult to change, and become detrimental to progress. Moral standards are established. Individuals who break out of such standards receive the condemnation of the group. One can observe the customs, beliefs, and attitudes of a rural community and characterize it in a single sentence.

5. *A constellation of institutions and services rendered for the benefit of the people of the community.* All people are in need of certain services to maintain normal existence. For instance, everyone must have a basic way of making a living, a means of educating his children, a means of worship and religious expression, social contacts and recreation, communication with others through the voice

40

and written page, contact with a doctor and lawyer. Therefore, there are six types of service which the community will supply in part or all together: (1) economic, (2) educational, (3) religious, (4) social, (5) communicative, and (6) professional. Most of these needs are supplied through organized services rendered to people.

The above mentioned services may be considered "life-support systems." By life-support is meant "essential to life." The individual must have available in some form each of the systems. He may be forced to travel a number of miles from his residence to obtain the service; it may be poorly supplied; and if it is not available, it will be necessary to seek residence where the service is available. This is the primary force behind mass migration of people bringing with it the depletion or increase of a population. A brief description of each of the major life-support systems is presented. These are aspects of both rural and urban societies.

1. A community must offer its residents resources for making a living. There must be adequate job opportunities, a soil strong enough to support its owner or renter, or businesses or industries in which one can sell one's services. Without adequate economic resources, community structure soon disintegrates.

2. All people stand in need of education. Formalized education has been provided for in the development of an intricate program of public education. Community life consists of opportunities to educate children, youth, and adults. Through special programs of adult education, a continual development of the intellect should be provided.

3. Religious needs have been a part of every civilization since the beginning of the history of man. The community must provide, through its institutions, opportunities for worship and the expression of one's religious faith.

4. Social relationships are as deeply rooted in the human structure as religious desires. All people have the herd instinct. They want to associate with friends; they want to do things together during leisure hours. The community structure must consider this fact and provide opportunities for such association. Commercialized social and recreational activities have become a part of the American culture. The movie house, the park, swimming pool, and less desirable forms of commercialized recreation are a part of the community structure.

5. All communities must provide resources for communication of its people within the group. Transportation facilities must be adequate. Road systems in our modern culture are proving to be a decided pattern of rural community development. The telephone communication is an important function of community structure. With the breakdown of the rural telephone system since 1920 and the refusal of public utility companies to rebuild rural lines, the rural electrification cooperatives have moved into the area of building a strong communication system among rural people. The weekly town newspaper has been a source of important rural community communication.

The urban transportation problem is major in most cities. Congestion on the freeways and streets in rush morning and evening traffic is an increasing problem. Systems of mass transit are still to be satisfactorily developed. With the factory being built away from the center of the city the person who can not afford to own a good automobile is in difficulty as public transportation facilities are often inadequate.

6. Professional services must be available for all people. There are legal matters which require the services of a lawyer, physical needs requiring the services of a doctor, religious needs requiring services of a minister. In the

community structure these needs must be provided for. One of the difficulties facing the small rural community is the fact that professional people have refused to live among and serve rural people. This phenomenon is one of the deciding factors in the development of the enlarged community structure described below.

With the above definition of a rural community and the six types of services rendered by that community before the reader, it will be seen immediately that it is not possible for each rural community to have all of the these services available. Therefore, to a certain extent, the number of services in a community determines the size of the community. Communities, then, are classified in various categories. According to Kolb and Brunner there are five types, dependent upon the extent of the services provided to the constituent members of the community:

1. *Single service community.* This is composed of people living in a village and open country with only one of the six services available. This is an elementary school, a church, or a general store. Seldom does such a community consist of more than two hundred people in the village center.

2. *Limited service type community.* More than one service, but not all six, are offered and made available in the community structure. It is a village (and the territory surrounding it) of two hundred to five hundred inhabitants. Approximately 80 percent of the trade of such a community center is drawn from the area outside the central village.

3. *Semicomplete service type community.* The central village or town of five hundred to one thousand inhabitants offers most of the six major services, but not necessarily all. Approximately 75 percent of the trade in the central town is drawn from the surrounding area.

4. *The complete, partially specialized service type community.* The central town is composed of one thousand to five thousand inhabitants. It offers to its residents all six services and may offer some specialized services, such as a small hospital. It may be the county seat town with several lawyers. There may be small factories, advanced opportunities for learning, recreational facilities, and so forth. Approximately 50 percent of the trade of the town is drawn from the surrounding community rural area.

5. *The urban or highly specialized service community.* All six services are offered in the community center, plus fields of specialization in all areas.[7]

Karl A. Fox and T. Krishna Kumar hold to a concept which relates the size of a town or city to the economic services supplied. The following classifications are given:

> First, there is the *full convenience center,* typically of 1,000 to 2,500 population and from $1,000,000 to $5,000,000 annual volume of retail sales. Second, there is the *partial shopping center* of 2,500 to 5,000 population and about $5,000,000 to $10,000,000 of retail sales. A good many of the small- and medium- sized countyseat towns in Iowa would fall in this category. Third, there is the *complete shopping center,* typically of more than 5,000 and less than 25,000 population with $10,000,000 to $40,000,000 of retail sales.[8]

The services rendered in the community center become the means of drawing the boundary lines of the community outreach. This is discussed more fully in chapter 8. It is sufficient to state that the rural community is composed of a geographic area with one village or town surrounded by several rural neighborhoods. The central town is the center of common activities, from which the people of the area derive for the most part their primary or day-by-day services.

In the structure of modern rural life, the community is vitally important as a social unit. The development of a strategy for a church in the community setting, considering natural affinities, is one of the tasks of the church. It is possible, for instance, to develop a program within one community structure that could not be developed between two communities. To attempt a program of closely integrated work in two communities is to invite defeat. Churches attached together for consolidation, extended ministry, enlarged charge, yoked field, or federated church should be in the same community for harmony. There is frequently a high degree of jealousy and competition between contiguous rural communities. Athletic contests, the competition for business, competition for receiving county or state aid for maintaining public schools or roads—all lead to friction between communities. Such friction inevitably creeps into the church and can spell defeat in cooperative programs. *A clear comprehension of the neighborhood and community concept is one of the first essentials for the development of a strong program of the church in town and country areas.*

Locality Group III: The Enlarged Community

The third sociological unit in rural society is the enlarged community. To date, there has been little scientific research on the enlarged community comparable to that for the rural neighborhood and community. This is, no doubt, because it is a rather recent development, and has come with the consolidation of schools and good highways. An enlarged community consists of two or more rural communities bound together in a natural or political area, with a dominant town in which all communities have a common interest. This is frequently synonymous with a county or part of a county. Figure 1 maps the typical rural neighborhood, rural community, and enlarged community.

There are many things which draw rural people together within the county structure. All people have the same county government. Services of the county agricultural agencies are at the command of all people in the county. School supervision, even to a county school board, is established on a wider perspective than the local community. Consolidation of high schools has brought the mind of the people to think beyond their local area. There are some sociologists who now feel the rural county—that is, a

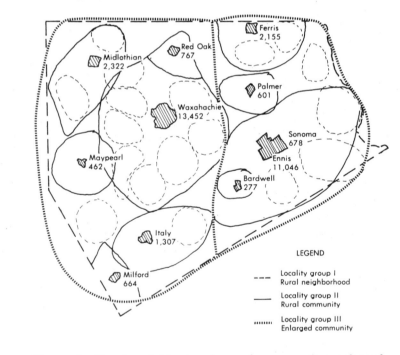

Figure 1. Rural neighborhood, rural community, enlarged community in Ellis County, Texas, with towns and cities and 1970 population.

county with the central town no larger than twenty-five hundred people—is becoming more community-like. In other words, the qualities of community as described above are applicable to the entire county. Approximately one-half of the counties in the United States, or fifteen hundred, fall in this classification.

There are hundreds of counties in the nation which have towns of more than twenty-five hundred population which are still rural in their outlook. Many counties have towns of five thousand, ten thousand, or even twenty thousand which are dependent primarily upon the agricultural operations in the surrounding area for their major economic activities. These counties, though not rural in the technical sense as defined by the U.S. census, are rural in outlook. Enlarged communities are formed around such towns, and become important administrative units for the church.

For all practical purposes in rural church administration, the county serves as the basis of study. Population data, information on housing, agriculture, business, and industry can be secured on the county basis. These are areas of cooperation in church work by all churches in the county which cannot be accomplished by churches in adjoining counties. One must always be mindful of the rural community structure within a county, however, and recognize there are limitations to what can be done beyond the rural community. In subsequent chapters, organizational procedures within the enlarged community area will be discussed. With approximately one-half of the counties in the United States classified as rural, one can readily see how important this unit is in the structure of nonmetropolitan America.

Natural barriers, such as rivers, lakes, mountains, and forests, may divide a county into two or more enlarged community groups. Another factor may be the existence of two towns of almost the same size. If there is, for example, a town of two thousand population which is the county seat and a town of twenty-five hundred which is not the county seat, there most likely will be much friction between them. This may make it impossible for the two towns to work together.

Other counties may have a larger town, up to ten thousand population, and a subordinate town of twenty-five hundred. It is possible that an enlarged community would be around each of these towns, or one of them, not including the other. Therefore, it may be said that *the enlarged community consists of one dominant town with one or more subdominant towns and their surrounding rural neighborhoods, bound together by natural, political, or trade affinities.*

Locality Group IV: The Functional Economic Area

In recent years there has emerged a fourth meaningful locality group in nonmetropolitan areas, the functional economic area (hereafter referred to as FEA). Some of the most extensive work on the FEA has been done by Karl A. Fox in the department of economics at Iowa State University of Science and Technology and his colleagues in economics and sociology. Fox has used Charles J. Galpin's concept of the trade-area community of 1911-13 which was published in a bulletin, "The Social Anatomy of an Agricultural Community," [9] and has applied it to the contemporary scene with good roads and rapid automobile transporation. Galpin held that a town would draw persons in the countryside to it for various types of trade and services. If within a county there were several towns, each would have around it a trade area which would become a

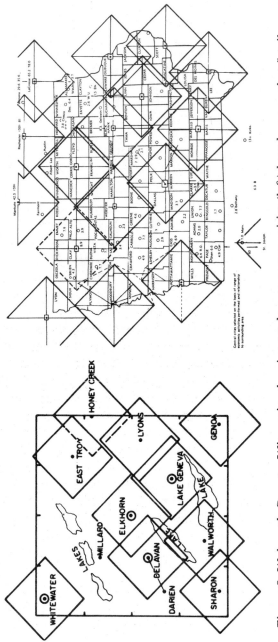

Figure 2. Walworth County, Wisconsin, showing trade area communities (left) based on travel at 5 miles per hour defined by C. J. Galpin in 1915; and the State of Iowa major trade areas (right), functional economic areas, based upon travel at 50 miles per hour. "Schematic Map . . ." by C. J. Galpin . . ." and Fifty-Mile Communting Distances . . ." from *Change in the Small Community*, edited by William J. Gore and Leroy C. Hodapp (copyright 1967. Friendship Press, New York, used by permission), pp. 76, 79.

community. Due to slow transporation and poor roads in 1913, the trade area was limited to approximately a one-hour travel distance, or a radius of approximately five miles. Using the state of Iowa for research, Fox has shown how there are major cities which serve an economic area or an approximate fifty-mile radius, or one-hour travel time on good roads by automobile. A rectangle is used rather than a circle because roads are laid out on section lines rather than diagonally. In other words, one would have to travel so many miles east or west and so many miles north or south to reach the city. Fox draws the conclusion, then, that the entire state of Iowa could be compared with Galpin's Walworth County, and the seventeen FEAs of the state of Iowa and its bordering cities in the neighboring states could be compared with the ten trade area communities of Walworth County (see Figure 2).

The FEA then becomes the center for major marketing trade, specialized services, higher education, and employment. Fox contends that people will travel one hour or fifty miles in one direction for such services.

For the purposes of church administration the FEA can become a meaningful planning area for denominational and interdenominational work. At this time it is too large an area to think of for cooperative parishes, but it has significant meaning in regard to a base to start from for regional church planning. Some church planners envision the FEA as the basic unit in the future for the ecumenical church in nonmetropolitan areas. Most states are now divided into such areas.

Meaningful Locality Groups in Metropolitan Areas

Some Theories of Urban Development

It is beyond the scope of this writing to go into detail in regard to the structure of the city. It is necessary, however, to examine some aspects of the nature of the city in order to assist in knowing where cooperative parishes may be effective in church administration.

Urban sociologists have developed a series of concepts which may help in defining the nature of the city. Four basic concepts are stated:

1. *Centralization.* There is a tendency for persons in the city to concentrate their interests, seek fulfillment of their needs, and to perform economic functions in a basic center or centers within the city. This may result in the central business district, the hub of city activities.

2. *Decentralization.* Decentralization is the tendency to move away from a center, dispersing interests of persons in a number of places rather than one. The modern city is marked by decentralization. A person may avoid for years

either overtly or covertly going to the central business district of a city. Many centers of specialized services are dispersed throughout the modern city.

3. *Segregation.* There is a tendency for the city dweller, voluntarily or involuntarily, to find persons of similar interests, socio-economic levels, or racial or ethnic groups. Thus there are clusters of groups of rather homogeneous characteristics throughout the city.

4. *Invasion and succession.* When a segment of the city is characterized by persons moving out and different use of the land being adopted, this is known as invasion. A different group of persons will move into the area. This may be a different racial group, ethnic group, religious group, nationality, and/or socioeconomic group. When such a group completely displaces a former type of resident this is known as succession.[1]

Based upon the theories of urban concepts, there are three well-known basic theories of urban growth: E. W. Burgess' theory of concentric zones, Homer Hoyt's theory of sectors, and Harris and Ullman's multiple-nuclei theory. In each theory it must be recognized that they are inadequate descriptions, and none can be considered as an ideal type. They are attempts to formulate a method of understanding urban growth patterns, and each has fundamental principles of truth, but each has areas of error. They are described here to assist in understanding more fully the nature of the city, and to help in understanding in some instances, why cooperative parishes are useful in church administration.

Burgess' Concentric Zone Theory

Burgess held that there are five major areas of the city in a concentric-circle pattern:

1. The central business district characterized by office buildings, department stores, banks, hotels, restaurants, entertainment centers, and transportation centers. This is "down town" in most cities.

2. The zone of transition characterized by old residential housing being changed to multiple-family housing, heavily populated with low income people, immigrants, a mixture of racial and culture groups, social outcasts, criminals, and prostitutes. This area in more recent years has been termed the "inner city," whether located in the immediate zone around the central business district or an isolated ghetto at any part of the city. Numerous studies have been made of the inner city revealing it as characterized by the highest concentration of crime, communicable disease, mental problems, racial, ethnic, or nationality groups, and the lowest economic and educational levels.

3. The zone of the workingmen's home. The third circle, according to Burgess, was characterized by being the residence of the laboring man. Housing would be inexpensive, but not in a high state of deterioration.

4. The zone of the middle-class dweller. The fourth zone was characterized by better housing occupied by business and professional people. It also had, in Burgess' concept, better apartments and some hotels.

5. The commuters' zone. On the edge of the city live the persons of higher income with large yards and expensive housing. The residents commute to work daily making a "bedroom city" out of their area.[2]

Any city dweller can readily observe the validity of the Burgess theory, and also the inadequacy of it. Basically the theory states that there are definitely distinguishable areas of the city which are definable. The theory of invasion and succession is also understood more readily, as there is a tendency for population to move from the inner circle

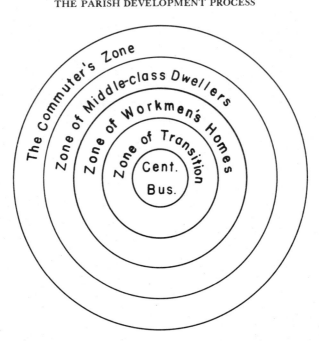

Figure 3. Burgess' concentric zone theory of urban development. *Source:* Robert E. Park, Ernest W. Burgess, R. D. McKenzie, *The City* (Chicago: University of Chicago Press, 1925). Copyright © 1925 by The University of Chicago Press,

to the outer when there is upward mobility in socioeconomic levels of a people. The present pressure being brought by governmental agencies on desegregation in housing and public schools is an illustration of an attempt to help persons break out of the class, ethnic, and racial barriers imposed by segregation and invasion.

Hoyt's Sector Theory of Urban Growth

Hoyt's theory is based primarily on the concept that rental values of residential property are the basic determining factors in distribution of socio-economic levels of residents. High rental areas tend to be located in one or more sections of the city, and in some cases, the low-rent areas are more or less like the shape of a cut of pie stretching across the zonal circles as described by Burgess. Hoyt held that transportation arteries, the terrain of the land, and such phenomena as lakes or water fronts make for distribution of socio-economic levels of culture.[3]

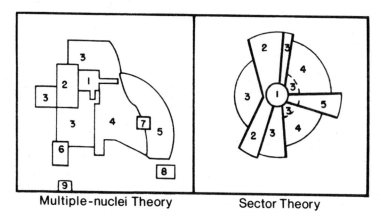

Multiple-nuclei Theory   Sector Theory

DISTRICT

1. Central business district
2. Wholesale light manufacturing
3. Low-class residential
4. Medium-class residential
5. High-class residential
6. Heavy manufacturing
7. Outlying business district
8. Residential suburb
9. Industrial suburb

Figure 4. Hoyt's sector theory of urban development; and Harris and Ullman's multiple-nuclei theory of urban development. *Source:* C. D. Harris and E. L. Ullman, *Annals* (November, 1945); Noel P. Gist and Sylvia Fleis Fava, *Urban Society,* 5th ed. (New York: Thomas Y. Crowell, 1964), p. 110.

Harris and Ullman's Multiple-Nuclei Theory

Harris and Ullman held that there are several centers or nuclei around which the residential and business activities of the city are developed. These are centers for retailing, wholesaling, finance, government, recreation, education, and so on. They held that similar types of businesses tended to cluster together and to isolate themselves from other businesses. Transportation becomes a major factor with railways, waterways, and major streets.[4]

It is sufficient at this point to state that transition and change are the ever-present dilemma of the city dweller. Decentralization is taking place rapidly in most American cities. The move to the suburbs is still major. Apartment living is increasing. Transition by invasion and succession is always going on. This leads to the restating of a basic thesis for the necessity of examining the cooperative ministry as a meaningful form of church administration. Where there has been a transition in racial, ethnic, nationality, or socio-economic level of a people, and there are existing older congregations, the cooperative parish may offer a means of effective church administration.

Locality Group V: The Urban Neighborhood

The urban neighborhood may be defined as a distinctive geographic area within a city which is predominantly residential, of near the same socio-economic level, in which there is an elementary school, some small businesses, one or more small shopping centers, and several churches. There is no distinctive interaction between the residents of the area as in the rural neighborhood. There is interaction on the institutional level, such as in public school activities, church relationships, and political wards or precincts. It has been estimated that approximately 90 percent of the Protestant churches in the city can be classified as neighborhood churches. Such churches will draw 60 or more percent of their members from within a one-mile radius of the church. A rule of thumb in urban church development has been to establish churches of the same denomination not closer than two miles apart, allowing each church a mile radius for the service area. Many planners feel this is too close, and with modern transportation, including expressways, churches need to be established on the basis of the major travel arteries and at a greater distance.

Within the city thousands of neighborhood churches have great difficulty in maintaining themselves. Some church planners feel a church needs to have five hundred members to have a leadership and economic base to sustain itself without being impoverished. This will vary with the economic level of the congregation, but it remains true that a church which is small usually has difficulty in meeting its budget and usually does not have sufficient leadership resources for an effective program. The pastor of the too-small church often feels the work is not challenging to his talents and abilities. He also is expected to do his own clerical work and carry the major administrative load. This will often lead to poor study habits and lack of sermon preparation resulting in poor preaching.

The urban neighborhood church many times needs the strength of other neighborhood churches within the region, both of the same and different denominations.

The urban neighborhood is in a constant state of change. The evolution of the urban neighborhood is described below:

1. The urban neighborhood is started by a land and housing developer who builds a group of houses of similar structures, size, and cost. This will attract homeseekers

who wish for pleasant surroundings in which to rear their families. They want neighbors of a similar socio-economic status. They visit with each other, care for each other's children, and engage in other practices which are commonly thought of as "neighboring."

2. As time passes new persons come into the neighborhood through transference of property, rental, new zoning regulations permitting business invasion, and so on. Neighboring becomes less and less, and the orbit of one's neighbors becomes smaller.

3. There may be invasion of racial or ethnic groups. Some houses may be converted to multiple housing. Neighborhood pride tends to decrease.

4. Finally personal contacts practically disappear. Neighboring is a thing of the past. The district loses its identity as a distinct neighborhood. It may continue to be a part of a respectable residental area. It may be changed into multiple housing with apartments replacing the single-family dwellings. It may degenerate into a slum or ghetto with a high rate of crime, delinquency, and other characteristics of the inverted neighborhood.

In the midst of the neighborhood there is the existing church. It has served well the growing population in the bright days of neighborhood solidarity, but faces increasing difficulty with the transition of the neighborhood. The new people of the neighborhood may not feel at home in the existing church. They may be of a different racial or ethnic group. They may be of a different socio-economic and educational group. As the older members of the church move out or die, the church becomes increasingly difficult to maintain.

Time of change from a newly begun neighborhood to the completely changed neighborhood is diffiiciult to determine. A rough estimate is between twenty and forty years. Zoning regulations, housing requirements, the "will of the city council" to maintain the stability of an urban neighborhood play a large part. In more recent years city planners have worked at preventing neighborhood deterioration and housing blight.

The basic thesis of this work is applicable in the changing neighborhood patterns: Where there has been a transition in racial, ethnic, nationality, or socio-economic levels of people, and there are existing older congregations, the co-operative parish may offer a means of effective church administration.

Locality Group VI: The Urban Community

The urban community is composed of two or more urban neighborhoods in which the socio-economic level of its residents is quite similar. There will be numerous churches of different denominations, several elementary schools, usually one junior high school, and one senior high school, though the schools may draw from several urban communities.

In the Council on Church Union's plan for the Church of Christ Uniting, the parish plan calls for the parish to be within the urban community. The parish would consist of one or more major centers and a number of sub-centers in church buildings and "house churches." The major conceptual idea is that a group of congregations would attempt an adequate and whole ministry to all persons within the parish. This is an adaptation of the larger parish and group ministry plans described in the following chapter.

The map, Figure 5, has urban neighborhoods and communities delineated.

In any attempt at organizing cluster groups, group

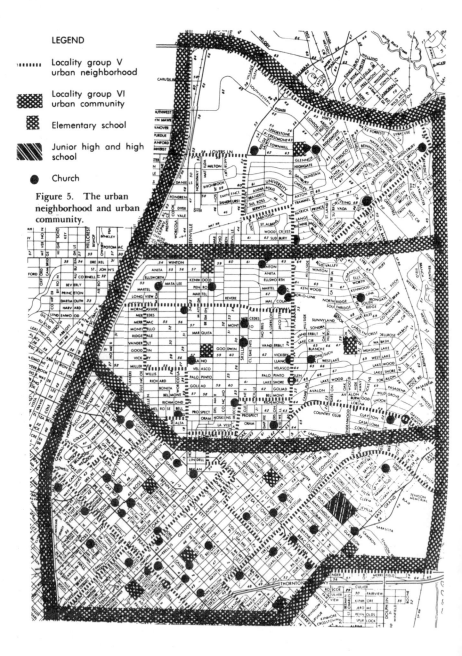

LEGEND

.... Locality group V
urban neighborhood

Locality group VI
urban community

Elementary school

Junior high and high
school

● Church

Figure 5. The urban
neighborhood and urban
community.

60

ministries, or larger parishes within the city the meaningful locality groups need to be defined. Some guidance on the process for delineation is discussed in chapter 8.

Community as a Social System

The term "locality group" has been used in this chapter because it refers to a specific geographic form or a territory which can be defined. For analytical and administrative purposes the descriptions are viable and meaningful. However, a trade area community (locality group II) or an enlarged community (locality group III) does not necessarily mean that there is a meaningful community in the sense of common understanding and fellowship. Writers in the field of community have attempted to formulate concepts of community which are not geographically limited, but which will include persons of like mind and interests.

Among other theories which have emerged is that of the community as a social system. Charles P. and Zona K. Loomis hold that various social theories in regard to human relations have been built around nine major elements of interaction:

> From among these aspects those that are considered elements are (1) belief (knowledge); (2) sentiment; (3) end, goal, or objective; (4) norm; (5) status-role (position); (6) rank; (7) power; (8) sanction; and (9) facility. At any given moment in time the structure of a given social system may be described and analyzed in terms of these elements.[5]

As one thinks of community as a social system, Loomis' concepts can serve for analytical purposes:
1. *Belief* (knowledge) is centered around what one holds as ultimate truth, or that which is of vital importance. Belief may carry with it a sense of destiny or ultimate reality.

2. *Sentiment* conveys the concept of "how one feels about it." Values placed upon certain things, loyalties created and understood.

3. *End, goal, or objective* indicates the concepts of persons involved as to what they consider to be their purpose in life along with other persons. As common goals or objectives arise, a sense of oneness with others is developed.

4. *Norms* are established by every group of people. They are inherited from a preceding culture, altered by individual desires, fused with other cultures, but are usually fairly well understood by a body of people of like mind.

5. *Status-role* (position) indicates what is held by the body of people to be symbols of attainment with a hierarchy of values.

6. *Rank* implies a hierarchy of positions within a culture which are assigned to leaders and followers within the society.

7. *Power* refers to authority which is invested in persons or in the system for decision-making, action, enforcement of sanctions, and bringing into being that which is best for the group.

8. *Sanctions* are self-imposed disciplines of a body of people for control of the persons within the group. Sanction implies rewards for certain achievements and disciplines for infraction of the understood standards of the group.

9. *Facility* implies the process by which the group is able to attain its ends, goals, and objectives and to operate as a social system. It may imply government, a constitution, authority, leadership, understood roles, and positions.

From the brief analysis above, it can be observed that wherever the nine criteria exist, there exists a social system. It does not limit the social system to a geographic location, though it does not exclude such from the definition.

The social system as described is applicable in any section of society, rural or urban. A city ghetto may have each of the characteristics. They may exist in a city residential area or in suburbia. They are frequently far more important in church planning than just geography.[6]

IV

Cooperative
Parish Structures

The word "parish" is defined by Webster in two manners: (1) a religious congregation comprising all those who worship together in one church; also, the district in which they live; (2) the ecclesiastical district committed to the pastoral care of one clergyman. In these two definitions we have summed up the concept of parish as it is normally thought of in the United States. The word "parish" conveys the idea of a local congregation but also of a territory around a local church for which that congregation has responsibility. In England the parish idea conveys the concept that the parish priest or vicar is responsible for ministering to all the persons who live within a certain geographic region. This concept is conveyed through the Roman Catholic Church and is adhered to in that when a Catholic family moves from one parish to another, it is expected to change membership. The Protestant churches in America with their spirit of freedom have never adhered strictly to this concept. Parish lines may be drawn for administrative purposes, but by and large, all persons who are members of the church have the right to belong to any church of their choice. Without a state church or a strong ecclesiastical overarching body to enforce parish structure, the freedom of choice concept will remain in American life.

By parish we are thinking of that territory for which a denominational or interdenominational program of church work should have planning and administrative responsibility. This may consist of a rather small area or a comparatively large area, depending upon density of population, the potential for mission, and the natural sociological groupings as described in chapters 2 and 3. Too many congregations and pastors conceive of the work of their church as being limited to its present constituency. In other words, many people are left out of the parish because they have not made an overt attempt to become a part of an organized membership. If we can bear in mind the broader concept of parish, then we can look forward to various types of organizations to perform a ministry of greater service to all persons who are within the geographic area under consideration for ministry. Several types of organizations are presented in some detail in order to present a clearer definition of the parish ministry. All types are applicable to rural and urban church administration.

The Consolidated Church

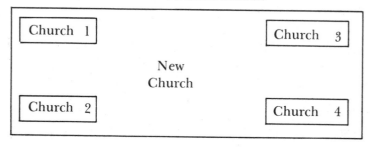

The consolidated church consists of two or more congregations of the same, or of different, denominations that work out an agreement of consolidation whereby a new congregation is brought into being. In some cases a new building is erected, or in other cases two or more buildings are put together to form a more substantial building. In some cases a church will consolidate with another existing church and be absorbed into the membership of that church. In this case the building of the church into which the congregation is moving will become the home for the new congregation.

Through recent years there has been a tendency on the part of many persons in small, open country churches to rebel against the concept of consolidation. It has in many cases been a rebellion against the encroachment of authority from the outside and a feeling of animosity, particularly toward those persons located in towns. In more recent years, however, the animosities of rural and urban people have been diminished until in many cases there is much cooperation taking place prior to a time of consolidation of the churches. There is much precedent in our public school systems in America for consolidation. There has been much rebellion against consolidation of schools in many sections of the country; but as consolidation has taken place, many persons have felt that the advantages of a larger school with a stronger teaching staff and more adequate building have been worth the price paid in giving up the individual oneroom schools. Sometimes, however, persons have felt that the autonomy of the individual was destroyed and that something went out of the neighborhood when the school left.

In recent years I have discovered many places where church consolidation has taken place with very little fanfare or pressure by denominational executives. Local congregations have come to realize that a neighborhood has disintegrated and the time for the open country church to move its constituency bodily into another congregation has come about. Frequently this has been a very happy situation which results in the retention of most of the people in the churches under consolidation.

A case in point is a small North Missouri congregation which voluntarily consolidated with a town church four miles away. On the consolidation Sunday a "victory service" was held in the country church consisting of a reading of the history of the church, rituals of praise, and a sermon by the denominational executive. At the close of the service the congregation went in one group and placed their membership in the town church. The rural building was sold at public auction, with the stipulation that it was to be razed within ninety days after purchase. The basement was then filled and the property returned to the heirs of the original donors. There was no cemetery.

In another case where there was a cemetery near the church, the building was sold for one dollar to the cemetery association with the stated purpose that it was to be preserved as a funeral chapel and place of memorial service. It was written into the title of the property that, should religious services other than memorial services be conducted, they were to be under the direction of the denomination which once housed the congregation. This was to prevent fly-by-night evangelists from using the building.

Consolidation should never be forced upon a neighborhood church. This cannot be said too strongly, for consolidation forced from the outside, or by denominational executives, causes great confusion and many times undue anxiety and antagonism. Studies have revealed that when a consolidation is forced, ordinarily only 10 to 20 percent of the people will cooperate in the consolidation. This leaves a large number of people to seek another church, or to remain unchurched. Similar studies have revealed that when consolidation comes from the inner desires of the congregation involved, 80 to 90 percent of the people will probably go along with the consolidation.

It has been estimated by persons in the field of research that approximately two thousand churches per year have been closing in rural areas across America for the past thirty years. This, no doubt, is a true estimate and more than an educated guess. The question remains: What happens to the people when a church closes? Are they left without a church, are they happily integrated into the life of another congregation, or are they consolidated into the life of one or more congregations? Throughout this work we have attempted to present the concept that the parish is the responsibility territory for some congregation. When a church ceases to be, there ought always to be some form or organization which is standing ready to minister to the persons in that geographic region. If consolidation is the answer, then there needs to be some kind of an overt method by which people will be brought into an understanding of one another. Some of the forms of cooperation described below are means of bringing persons into a vital relationship so that they understand one another sufficiently well to move together eventually toward consolidation. It is the belief of this author that if a rural church is needed to maintain neighborhood solidarity and a spirit of community among a people, even though the congregation may become quite small, there should be every effort to continue a partial ministry in the local church. It is possible that a partial ministry can be maintained in a local church and a fuller ministry in one of the cooperative ministries described below.

The Extended Ministry

Strong church	One pastor	Weak church

The extended ministry (sometimes called the extension church, the outpost, or other terms) consists of a strong church sharing its ministry with another church. In recent years in some sections of the nation the extended ministry has been the means of serving thousands of people who otherwise would have been isolated from a strong ministry. Frequently, a small country church finds itself orphaned because other churches on the pastoral charge have either ceased to be or have become strong enough to employ a pastor on a full-time basis. The small church is not strong enough to support a full-time pastor, and, even if it did have the financial resources, there would not be enough work for the minister to perform in being the pastor of such a small congregation.

The extended ministry is a process by which a strong church accepts the responsibility for ministering unto another church which is close enough for the pastor or staff to perform Sunday activities as well as weekday ministries. As has been described in chapters 2 and 3 dealing with the nature of society, many small churches have been established which now are five to ten miles from town. Good highways make it possible for a minister to be in a country church at an early hour and back in the town church within five to ten minutes' time for another service of worship. Again the concept of parish is brought to mind as the town church assumes the responsibility for serving persons within the geographic area by extending its ministry farther out into the countryside. The normal structure for such organization consists of: (1) one pastor, or pastor and employed staff; (2) two or more congregations under the direction of one pastor or staff; (3) a strong town or city church sharing its ministerial leadership with one or more churches. The second church may have a complete organization or a partial organization, depending upon size and leadership potential, and it should pay a proportionate share of the pastor's salary and denominational items.

Denominational bodies need to establish policies in regard to extended ministries and other forms of parish organization. This means that the denominational body needs to draw up specific statements concerning pastors who serve in extended ministries in regard to salary base and other remuneration. This is particularly true in episcopal forms of government where salary base becomes a major item in regard to appointments. The salary which is paid by the second church needs to be considered as a part of the basic total salary of the pastor; and when a pastor is brought into the new situation, it should be explained to him that the second church is a part of the pastoral appointment. Tragedy has resulted when this is not the case, and the pastor feels that he has had something added to his load after being appointed.

Sometimes one of the major problems that is faced in the extended ministry is the attitude of the congregation in the town church. Frequently, church leaders will say, "We have employed our pastor for our church, not for a second church." There is also in some areas of the country a stigma in that it is considered a lesser appointment for a minister to serve more than one congregation. Fortunately, in many cases, these attitudes have been overcome, and the town church recognizes a parish responsibility and is willing to share its pastor with the people in the second church.

In all likelihood the only part of the program of the church that the pastor will miss is some of the church school in the town church. Church schools traditionally have been lay organizations and should be able to stand on their own administrative leadership without having to demand the time of the pastor to be present. Thousands of rural churches for fifty years have maintained their Sunday schools without the assistance of a pastor, and in many cases the town church now can assume the leadership of the church school without the pastor's presence on Sunday morning. There is much to be gained by the consideration of the extended ministry by town and city churches across America as they extend their parish boundaries to include areas where there are small, open country churches and other churches nearby which need a ministry.

One of the most effective forms of church extension within a city is the extended ministry. A strong city church can share its ministry with a smaller church or a church in a different socio-economic, racial, or ethnic group. One member of the church staff can carry major responsibility for the extension church.

The Enlarged Charge
(Sometimes called the Larger
Charge or Cooperative Charge)

Church 1	One	Church 3
Church 2	pastor	Church 4

The enlarged charge consists of two or more congregations under the direction of one pastor operating as one unit with several places for services of worship. Again, the concept of the parish is brought into play as one thinks of an enlarged charge. The enlarged charge is a situation in which there are several congregations of one denomination, or of several denominations, which decide to cooperate in a program whereby they employ one pastor to serve all the churches. Rather than each church's functioning as a separate unit, however, they maintain their separate local buildings and localities, but actually perform the services of the church on a parish-wide basis. Autonomy is maintained in each local congregation, but cooperation is forthcoming in the total life and program of the total parish involving all congregations. The great advantages of such an arrangement lie in the fact that a fuller program of church activities can be promoted than can be done for individual congregations. The structure of an enlarged charge is given below:

1. There is an organization within each congregation consisting of official boards, various committees or commissions, women's work, men's work, youth work. The members of various organizations in the local congregations shall automatically be members of a charge-wide organization. In other words, the enlarged charge is organized as a single church would be, with separate executive bodies in each local congregation. For more effective work the local congregations may form a coordinated parish-wide organization and provide representatives for the parish-wide official board and other suborganizations. Coordinated planning shall be done on a parish-wide basis.

2. Each congregation shall have a budget consisting of local expenses, such as building maintenance, utilities, custodial service, insurance, and a sum to contribute to the parish-wide budget which shall include ministerial

support, missionary offerings, and other denominational expenses. A sum should be included in the latter for pastor's office and travel expense, a parish paper, parsonage or manse maintenance, and other parish-wide interests.

3. There shall be a central parish treasurer who shall receive from each local church the appropriate amount for the parish budget. The central treasurer shall disperse funds of the parish treasury consisting of ministerial support, missions, and other connectional items as well as parsonage expense, pastor's travel, office expense, and so forth. The budget described in item 2, which includes the ministerial support and denominational expenses as well as any item which concerns the entire parish, is sent to a central treasurer. The amount that each congregation shares in the total expenses of the parish is prorated on the ability of the congregation to pay rather than on the amount that the congregation receives of the pastor's time and ministry. Worship service schedules and other ministries of the pastor are worked out through the coordinating council.

4. As much as possible, overall planning and work shall be done on a parish-wide basis. For instance, the women's organization can be established on a parish-wide basis with circles in each local church. Training schools, youth activities, men's groups, evangelistic programs, and all other phases of the church can be planned on a parish-wide basis. There should be a parish paper distributed to all homes in all churches at least once a month.

One of the main advantages of an enlarged charge is the feeling that individuals receive by being a part of a dynamic whole. There is also the aspect of all the congregations serving all the people within the parish area. No longer is each congregation a separate unit; instead, each is a part of a total body attempting to serve all the people.

The Larger Parish

Probably the easiest way to define a larger parish is to refer back to the description of the enlarged charge and conceive of the charge being served by a staff of employed persons rather than one minister. Therefore, we would say that the larger parish is defined as an enlarged charge with these additional characteristics:

1. A multiple staff of ministerial and professional leadership serving all the congregations. The leadership may consist of assistant pastors, director of education, director of evangelism, and so forth.

2. There may be, though not necessarily, congregations of different denominations.

3. There will usually be a constitution controlling the work of the parish.

A brief history of the origin of the larger parish is recorded in chapter 1. Edmund deS. Brunner in his study of 1934 stated there are nine areas of concern which must be considered in establishing and maintaining larger parishes. These are sound principles which are applicable in present parish development.[1]

1. The territory included is an economic and/or social unit.

2. The territory has adequate resources, under normal economic conditions, in order to support the larger parish sooner or later.

3. The churches of the parish combine their finances, at least those regarding the salary of the staff and preferably for all items.

4. The staff consists of two or more persons with special training or interest in the field of responsibility to which each is assigned.

5. There is a functioning parish council.

6. The parish gives, or at least sincerely aims to give, many-sided service to the whole territory it serves and to every person within it.

7. The parish has exclusive possession of its field so far as Protestant work is concerned, or at least has cooperative relations with other religious groups and with community organizations.

8. The parish recognizes its interdenominational obligations.

9. The parish is assured of the continued support of the denomination or denominations concerned regardless of changes in administrative personnel.

In 1939 the New York State College of Agriculture produced a bulletin entitled *The Larger Parish, an Effective Organization for Rural Churches.* The bulletin was a condensation of the findings from a doctoral dissertation by Mark Rich. Three larger parishes were the basis of the study, but the entire scope of the larger parish movement was surveyed. The bulletin had widespread circulation and did much to foster the larger parish movement. Rich states, "A larger parish is a group of churches in a larger community or a potential religious community, working together through a larger parish council and a larger parish staff to serve the people of the area with a diversified ministry." [2] An examination of this statement reveals three fundamental ideas in the concept of a larger parish. (1) the community; (2) bona fide interchurch cooperation; and

75

(3) a specialization in training and service among the professional leaders.

In more recent times the larger parish has come to be accepted by many denominations as a means of serving a large constituency of people within a given geographic area with a multiple staff of trained leaders to bring a total and effective program of the work of the church to its constituents. A bibliography at the end of this work will contain other publications in the field of the larger parish.

The term larger parish, though originated in rural church administration near the beginning of this century, has been adopted in urban administration. Many inner city parishes are organized on the larger parish pattern. It may also be observed that the pattern for parish structures proposed by the Council on Church Union is basically the larger parish.

The Group Ministry

Charge 1 Pastor-director Church A Church B	Charge 2 Pastor Church A Church B Church C	Charge 3 Pastor Church A Church B Church C

The group ministry consists of two or more independent pastoral charges working cooperatively for the development of the work of the church in a given area. The group ministry is different from the larger parish in that each of the ministers in the group ministry is responsible for a pastoral charge of his own. Work is done on a cooperative basis rather than on a closely integrated, organized basis for all churches involved. The characteristics of a group ministry may be summarized as follows:

1. Two or more charges working cooperatively. It is best if the churches are located in one enlarged, rural community (locality group III—one dominant town and one or more subdominant towns). In cities the locality group will consist of one or more urban communities. (locality group VI).

2. A lay and ministerial council to guide the work of the organization is elected with representatives from each church.

3. Each minister serves a pastoral charge and derives his support from the charge.

4. There is a central budget for any unified program such as a newspaper, church and community worker, or other items of common concern.

5. A director is elected by the lay council or appointed by the appropriate denominational executive.

The group ministry had its origin in October of 1938 with the publication of a bulletin entitled "The Group Ministry," written by the late Aaron H. Rapking. Rapking had joined the staff of the Division of National Missions of the Board of Missions of The Methodist Church in 1938. He started to make a visual record of existing larger parishes in the United States and discovered that there was such diversity in the types of programs in operation that is was going to be virtually impossible to get any kind of documentation which would be meaningful. He called together a group of persons interested in the field of town and country church for consultation, and out of the consultation came the idea of the group ministry. Rapking summarizes his findings in the following quotation which is taken from correspondence.

In many town and country areas that have the same major trading, recreational, educational, and cultural centers there are from three to six Methodist ministers and from twelve to twenty-four churches.

Here is a word picture of my basic conception of the group ministry that I presented to the group: The appointment of our ministers to a regular charge in a recognized natural area such as a county seat town or trade center surrounded by communities and neighborhoods with the understanding that while they would do the work of a good minister of Jesus Christ on their charge, they would also work with other character building organizations to study and promote certain activities in the interest of coming to grips with the problems, the needs, and opportunities of the people and thus help bring the kingdom of God's ideals and attitudes into action in the total life of the area. One minister in the group might be strong in evangelism; another in dealing with people; while another's specialty might be that of promoting the redemptive process through Christian education. These ministers would meet every two weeks and with a map of the territory before them, study, pray, and plan to promote those projects and grapple with those problems, the solution of which would mean much to the building of the kingdom of God in the area and in the world.

As there is need for ministers to work together in a community or natural area, so there is great need for laymen and churches to join hands and work together to combat evil, promote, strengthen, and make more effective the program of the churches in the area. The establishing of a Methodist Fellowship Council did not call for a change in the present local or district church setup. The council would be established by electing one man, one woman, and one young person under twenty-four years of age from each church cooperating. The council should meet at least four times a

78

year. The ministers would be members of the council. Committees on survey, evangelism, Christian education, music, plays and pageants, stewardship, recreation, cooperation with other agencies could be appointed as needed.[3]

Though the term "larger parish" originated in the Congregational ministry and the term "group ministry" originated in The Methodist Church, both terms have become broader in their concept and scope and have been applied to any kind of work done in the general structure or pattern and with one or more denominations cooperating. It is interesting also to note that both terms have now been adopted by a number of denominations for work within city parishes. The latter is a revelation of the fact that the larger parish and group ministry are concepts of parish administration which are applicable in any area of ministry in metropolitan or nonmetropolitan areas. Within many cities the concept of group ministry has taken hold, not only in inner city but in all sections of the city. A case in point is a study by Douglas W. Johnson in 1966 titled *A Study of Methodist Group Ministries and Larger Parishes in the Inner City*. Johnson describes ten inner city parishes and uses the two terms "larger parish" and "group ministry." [4] It is also of interest to note that his first footnote reference is to Rockwell C. Smith's book *The Church in Our Town* (Nashville: Abingdon Press, 1955) and his second footnote reference is to my book *The Larger Parish and Group Ministry,* both books primarily treating the subject of rural church administration. Within a given geographic region which has some homogeneous continuity, six or eight churches are banding themselves together to do cooperatively what they cannot do individually. In many cases programs such as nursery schools, health clinics, the relief of those who are in physical need, and

79

joint programs of evangelism are undertaken. The cluster group, which has become popular in many cities, is a modified form of group ministry.

The Yoked Field

Church 1 Denomination 1	One pastor	Church 2 Denomination 2

The yoked field consists of two congregations of different denominations served by one pastor. Each church maintains separate budgets for denominational and missionary work, but cooperates on pastor's salary and mutual work.

The yoked field has proved to be quite valuable in areas in which the denominational programs have disintegrated to the point that there are not enough churches of one denomination to maintain a strong pastoral unit. By yoking together it is possible to call a minister to serve both churches with adequate salary and housing. Individual autonomy is retained by each congregation by its maintenance of its own denominational connections and support of its denominational programs.

The one problem that arises with the yoked field is determining what denomination will supply the ministry. It sounds good to say that one denomination will supply the ministry for four years and then the other denomination, for another four years. Congregations need to remember that ministers may find themselves in a predicament with their own denomination if they have stepped out of line of an ordinary pastoral situation. This is particularly true with persons in the episcopal form of government. Therefore, it is wise for the two churches to determine in advance which denomination they will ask to supply the minister. This denomination then becomes responsible for supplying the minister as long as the yoked field is in operation. It is possible that after a few years both churches will become a part of the one denomination which in reality is quite good if it can be done without too much friction. This, of course, is not the ultimate aim, but this sort of arrangement does sometimes eventuate.

The Federated Church

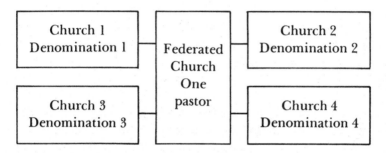

The federated church consists of two or more congregations of different denominations which unite to form one congregation under articles of federation. Within the United States in the last forty years there have been many churches which have federated. This has been done in cities where different denominational churches have united in one neighborhood in order to make a more effective ministry. It has been done in many small towns where there are three or four denominations competing with one another in a community that is strong enough to support one church, but not three or four. The federated church has had its successes and failures, like any other program of cooperative action. Some denominational leaders feel that it is not an effective way of solving the problems of the churches in town and country areas, while others feel that it is an effective type of organization and makes for good ecumenical action. With the rising impetus upon interchurch cooperation and the ecumenical movement, the federated church has the potential of strengthening the work of the church in many communities.

The federated church operates under articles of federation which in reality make up a constitution. The articles of federation define: (1) the method by which a pastor is selected; (2) the conditions of church membership and dismissal from the congregation; (3) the adoption of rituals for receiving members into the church, baptism, the Sacrament of the Lord's Supper, the solemnization of matrimony, and the burial of the dead (ordinarily such rituals are taken either from the denomination of one of the cooperating churches or one of the various ecumenical rituals that have now been produced); (4) directives regarding church school literature; (5) directives in regard to the appropriation of missionary funds; (6) denominational cooperation of the various denominations involved.

It can be seen that with so many areas in which some kind of consensus of opinion must be established by all the cooperating bodies that there are many opportunities for friction and discord in the federated church. The building alone sometimes proves to be a stumbling block. Which congregation will give up its building to meet in another? What will be done with the buildings that are abandoned? Some of the most effective federated churches have met the problem by moving the buildings bodily to the site of one, or to an entirely new site, and uniting them in the major plant of operation. In some cases all buildings have been abandoned, and a new building has been erected.

One of the major problems that is faced in the federated church, like that of the yoked field, is the problem of which denomination will provide a ministry. Again, it looks good in the articles of federation to provide that each denomination shall supply a pastor for a stated period of time in a rotating system. But again, the pastors who are willing to accept such a temporary arrangement may find it difficult at the end of their term in office to be brought back into line in their own denominations. It is far better if the articles of federation will state that one of the cooperating denominations is to supply the pastor from the beginning and for all time.

Many years ago the Iowa Council of Churches established in their comity committee a rule of thumb that they would assist any local Iowa community in establishing a federated church, provided the local community would ask the comity committee to make a study of the community and determine which denomination should then be responsible for supplying a ministry. This actually takes the responsibility out of the hands of the local people. This has worked quite effectively in several situations in the state.

The federated church has not served its day and should be considered as one of the means of cooperation in communities that are strong enough to support one church but not several.

Two Congregations in One Building

Congregation 1 Pastor and staff
Congregation 2 Pastor and staff

An emerging pattern of cooperation especially in urban churches is two congregations in one building. This is especially applicable in an older section of a city as a racial or ethnic population moves into the neighborhood. Language may be a problem making it essential that a bilingual ministry be available. Frequently the minority group is too small to employ a pastor and acquire housing. An existing church can put a bilingual person on its staff and provide housing for the minority congregation. Riverside Church in New York has provided a ministry of this type for Puerto Ricans for many years. This type of ministry is especially effective in the Southwest with an increasing Mexican American population. A United Methodist church in Dallas, Texas now has a Korean congregation and minister in the building belong to the Anglo-white congregation. A graduate student in Christian education used as her thesis the development of a church school curriculum in the Korean language considering traditional customs. There are unlimited possiblities in this form of church co-operation.

V

Establishing
The Cooperative Parish

Basic Principles of Parish Development

Cooperative parish development within local congregations is one of the most exacting, painstaking, and time-consuming tasks of church leaders. There are no shortcuts. All the known principles of group leadership, group dynamics, and group decision-making must be brought into focus in the light of a good theology of the church as a group of congregations is developed into a cooperative parish. Good planning and procedures will save defeat and blundering.

Let me illustrate the point. I was asked to sit in a session consisting of the employed staff and the advisory council of an inner city parish. The parish had been operating for three years and was fraught with many problems. The problems revolved around interpersonal relations between staff members, a lack of enthusiastic support of the congregations involved, a confusion as to the major task of the parish, poor job descriptions for the staff, and many other related areas. I listened to the discussion for two hours. I finally ventured to say that the basic problem lay in the fact that there had been little preparation for the establishing of the parish. Denominational leaders felt the need for the parish. They gathered together from various boards and agencies sufficient funds to rent a storefront building and employ a director (a white man in an almost 100 percent Negro community). It became the director's task to recruit the cooperation of the pastors and congregations in the area along with an old, well-established community settlement house which had been operated by an independent women's group. After a few minutes' discussion of the process of parish development, one of the women on the council spoke with insight. "I now see our problems. We were organized from the top down [cupping her hand above her head palm down] instead of being developed from the bottom up [she cupped her hand palm up at her side]." She had caught the most significant aspect of parish development. It must be a development of the people from the bottom up not from the top down.

In many years of assisting with parish development, this factor remains the most difficult for me to help leaders grasp. All too often a well-meaning pastor or a denominational executive, such as a district superintendent or executive secretary of a city board of missions or a chairman or executive of a denominational town and country commission, will see the need for a cooperative parish. He arbitrarily sets up the machinery for the parish and selects the leader. Little consultation is done with existing leaders and local congregations. The parish may develop if the selected leader has the ability to move cautiously and consultatively with congregations and ministers. Even if he is successful in gaining support, his work and the work of the parish will have been delayed many months and even years because of poor planning. In most cases poor planning will result in such negative reactions on the part of laymen that they will fail to give support, and the parish as such will have a dismal beginning and end in disaster.

On the positive side of parish development there are several fundamental principles which need to be thoroughly mastered:

1. *Employed church or parish staff and organizational structure are for the purpose of assisting the laity to be the church in worship, nurture, and at work in the world.* This is a partial statement of the theology of the church. The primary aim of a cooperative parish is to provide a structure through which the layman may find a full expression of personal Christian life in the corporate body of believers. Organization as an end in itself can become idolatry. It is only a means to an end.

2. *Persons will accept new ideas if they feel they are to their advantage.* This may sound somewhat mundane, but what holds true for physical utilities of life such as food, clothing, housing, gadgetry, is also true in religion. A major industry in America is advertising, which is primarily geared to convincing the individual that it is to his advantage to use product one over product two. When the individual is convinced of the fact, he will shift products even though he must use easy credit to do so.

When laymen have been helped to see the advantages of a cooperative parish over their current type of church work, they are ready to make the shift to adopt new plans. It is not a selling job; that would be manipulation. It is a task of informing and assisting the layman to be creative on his own thinking concerning his own ministry and the work of his church. Parish development in this sense is people development.

3. *Persons tend to support ideas they have had a share*

in formulating. Here again is a fundamental principle, which must not be ignored. In the entire process of parish development the consultative procedures need to be used. The role of the leader in developing a cooperative parish is that of a teacher, a coordinator, a catalyst; there is information given, ideas coordinated, and a pulling together of ideas to assist persons in gaining direction.

4. A fourth principle which needs to be observed is *allow freedom for the creative presence of the Holy Spirit.* Creativity is one of the greatest God-given attributes of mankind. God made men and women to be creative. He gave them the physical characteristics to be able to create new life in their own image. He gave them the ability to create ideas and the ability to put ideas into practice, taking the form of architecture, literature, art, inventions, organizations, business enterprises, more productive means of agriculture, educational institutions, and churches. The creative imagination of a group of laymen and ministers within a given geographic area needs to be turned loose under the influence of the Holy Spirit to bring into being the form and structure for ministry which will meet the needs of the people within the area. God is still creating!

The following discussion is a formal description of the scientific process for assisting a group of people to enact change in a given situation. This will be followed by a simple description of the process by which a parish can be developed incorporating sound principles of leadership as described above.

A Formal Process for Parish Development

One of the most concise and descriptive analyses of the process of social change is that devised by George M. Beal and his associates at Iowa State University of Science and

Technology. The diagram, Figure 14, gives a framework for social action. It is suggested that one read through the diagram from the left to right and then return to the following description for an understanding of the chart.

The numbers 1,2,3,4. etc., represent the steps in social action with each step being a foundation for the next step. There are, in addition to the stages in social action, some important considerations which run throughout the various stages. These are listed A,B,C, etc. Now to consider the stages:

1. The social systems. All social action takes place within the context of existing social systems. For our consideration we think of the church itself as a social system, and we also think of the area in which the church is located. The areas are described in chapters 2 and 3 as locality groups I through VI. In addition to the church and the locality groups there are subsystems such as power structures, formal and informal groups, social stratifications, governments, and interrelated areas of each.

2. Convergence of interests. All social action begins when the interest and definition of need on the part of two or more people converge and are brought together. Usually convergence of interest begins with a small group of people. In the case of the church this can be two or more laymen, two or more ministers, a minister and one or more laymen, denominational executives, a regional church body such as a board of missions or town and country commission. In other words, the convergence of interest may be stimulated by people within the system (church or churches) or persons from without the system (district superintendent, regional missionary, executive secretary for a regional church board, and so forth). Once there has been a convergence of opinion, there needs to be some tentative definition of goals which are sufficiently

defined and agreed upon for continued social action and exploration.

3. Analysis of the prior social system. In most situations there will be existing churches, remnants of past churches, or past traditions that need to be examined. Traditional patterns of successful and unsuccessful communication and cooperation will have been established. At this stage the persons seeking change (change agents) need to ask the following questions: (a) Has there in the past been a similar kind of project proposed? Was it successful? If so, what factor contributed to its success? If it was not successful, why not? The intent of these questions is to capitalize on former successes and to avoid former mistakes. (b) What types of cooperative projects have the people in the area undertaken before? What was their success, and how were they brought about? Such projects could be school consolidation, organization of a cooperative or a community council, and similar movements. (c) What is the general attitude of the people in the area toward progress? Is there a defeatist attitude, or are people optimistic about change? (d) What churches seem to work best together? Is there ill feeling between some churches which may prevent them from working together on a cooperative basis?

4. Delineation of relevant social systems (local churches and church bodies). Very few cooperative parishes will include all the churches of all the denominations within the area. It is well to study the churches of the area to see how many and which ones are needed in the cooperative parish to meet the needs or goals looked for. Some congregations will automatically eliminate themselves due to denominational policies. Other congregations will not feel the need for a cooperative parish, but the group promoting the investigation may feel they are needed. Both those churches which are interested in, and those

opposed to, a cooperative parish need to be taken into consideration and invited to participate in the process. Denominational executives such as bishops, district superintendents, area directors, executive secretaries of area boards and agencies need to be brought into the early stages of planning. Their attitude toward the project must be known and taken into account.

5. The initiating set. Up to this stage only a few persons have been involved, and they have operated primarily through conversation and without authority. An "initiating set" needs, now, to be selected. In initiating a cooperative parish, the initiating set can be selected by electing or appointing a small delegation, one to three persons, from each congregation. Other strategic persons such as pastors and denominational representatives will need to be on the initiating set or planning committee.

6. Legitimation. Legitimation is used here mainly in the sense of giving sanction for action. The sanction may be formal authority or an understanding for action. Within the initiating set described in step 5, there will be persons who are influential in a community action program such as the development of a cooperative parish. Such persons may or may not be influential people for other community action projects, but it is well to know where they stand in regard to their influence with persons in their respective congregations. Every church and community has influential persons who, in a sense, are the decision-makers for their group. Such persons can be instrumental in the success or failure of a cooperative parish because of the personal influence they have with the members of the congregation.

7. The diffusion set. At step 7 of the social action process more people are brought into the planning. The initiating set or committee from each church will now need to convey the information back to the local congregation of

what has taken place thus far. It is a good time to inform local church official boards and as many members of the congregation as possible of the planning to this stage. It is also a good time for evaluation to take place of what has been done so far and exploration of what further steps need to be taken. A sound principle for social action has been suggested as five Ps: Prior Planning Prevents Poor Performance.

8. Definition of need by more general relevant groups and organizations. This step is a broadening of the base of knowledge for persons who are to be involved in the cooperative parish. It calls for: (a) basic education of all persons to be involved in the parish. This is done through house groups where small groups of laymen are invited to participate in discussions, newsletters, public press, discussion in church school, and other church gatherings; (b) a questionnaire to all families involved, asking for basic information concerning the family, community activity participation, the work of each church and its effectiveness in the community, and so forth; (c) a look at other similar cooperative parishes as a means of stimulating action. Lay speakers from other successful cooperative parishes may be helpful.

9. Decisions (commitments) to action by each congregation. Each congregation is given the opportunity to vote on whether it will become a participating group in the cooperative parish. If thorough planning has taken place, congregations will be ready to make the decision for cooperation. At this stage there is still enough flexibility for much work is yet to be done, and congregations need to understand that they will have a part in setting up the final form or organization. They, at this stage, are committed to an idea with somewhat of an on trial participation.

10. Formulation of objectives.
11. Decision on means to be used.
12. Plan of work.
13. Mobilizing resources. Representatives from each participating congregation need to formulate the definite objectives of the group organization and to establish a framework by which the objectives can be attained. This will, in all likelihood, result in a constitution and bylaws to give direction to the parish. (See a sample constitution in Appendix A.) The constitution will give a general framework of organization, responsibilities, financial support, communications, committee structure, and so forth.

14. Action. The final stage is action. The cooperative parish comes into being and begins functioning as a parish.

15. Evaluation. At every stage careful evaluation needs to be made by examining progress and next steps. After a parish has functioned for a few months, the evaluation process needs to be brought into focus. Mistakes will be made, and the earlier they are caught, the better. It will be discovered that there are areas of need which have not been provided for. The parish council and the parish staff need to be in a constant state of evaluation to be sensitive to emerging needs.

In the chart will be seen a series of ABCs under the heading Continuing Processes and Considerations. These involve preparation of organizational structures, continuity of the organization, research and analysis, mobilizing resources, discovering leadership in each church, and the changing of social action at any stage in the process. The above areas need to be considered throughout the entire process. Chapter 8 is devoted to the necessary research in planning the cooperative parish.

Needless to say, the above process is long and detailed.

The human mind is often slow in accepting new ideas. The democratic process is designed to gain the opinion, knowledge, and strength from the largest number of persons possible for the support and work in the cooperative parish.

Social planning, which in our context means planning by church bodies, has been defined as a conscious process of personal interaction combining investigation, discussion, agreement, and action in order to achieve those conditions, relationships, and values regarded as desirable.[1]

An Informal Process for Parish Development

Keeping in mind the formal process for parish development the basic principles are applied to the local church situation with a less formal description. The process is applicable in the development of any of the types of cooperative parishes. The more congregations which are involved the more complicated the process becomes, and equally, the more necessary it is that the process be followed in its exact form.

The diagram, Figure 15, is a simplified description of the process with specific application to the development of a cooperative parish. It is suggested that the reader study the diagram, then study Appendix C, "Parish Development Aids," and then continue reading from this point.

Stage 1 is the initiation. Someone has to be initiator of the idea of a cooperative parish. This may come from within the potential parish or from without. Within the parish it will be a layman or a pastor. From outside the potential parish it will be a denominational executive such as a district superintendent, regional executive, board of missions, town and country committee, special task force appointed by a board or agency to study the area, or a general church agency.

2. Temporary geographic area. The initiator in consultation with other persons will arbitrarily determine the potential area for the cooperative parish. This will be one or more locality groups as described in chapters 2 and 3 of this book. As the study progresses it may be advisable to alter the geographic boundaries as it is discovered there are conditioning factors which were not apparent at the beginning.

3. Possible congregations and church institutions. As far as possible the potential churches and institutions within the area need to be determined. It is better to include churches and institutions which later may decide not to participate than to leave them out and ask them later to join the discussions. By institutions is meant primarily community centers, storefront missions, or any religiously oriented service group.

4. A meeting of pastors and key leaders. The initial meeting is purely exploratory. It needs to be quite informal with precaution that it must be stressed that no decisions have been made or will be made in the leadership group. Final decision for action will be in the existing congregations and institutions.

The meeting of the leaders may consist of just the pastors of the local congregations and employed executives of the institutions. In some cases this is advisable. Pastors may feel threatened by such a discussion, or they may feel free in a peer group to express their feelings. It is also observed that in a denomination with the episcopal form of government congregations expect their pastors to take initial steps. On the other hand, if we remain true to our doctrine of the church already expressed, the earlier laymen are brought into planning the better.

5. Leaders discuss the possibilities with church bodies. It must again be emphasized that no decisions have been made and final decision for action will be made in the local congregations. Frequently small congregations especially in rural areas are quite suspicious of larger congregations, feeling the motivation of the larger church is to absorb the small church in their membership. This is a critical time in parish development. The four basic principles stated earlier in this chapter must be observed, or the progress in development will be severely impared.

6. Each body gives approval for continued discussion and elects representatives. Each congregation or institution within the potential parish will now officially approve the idea of proceeding with discussion. They will elect from two to five persons to represent their congregation or institution. The representative along with the pastors and institutional executives and any related denominational executive will comprise a committee or task force to explore the possibilities for some type of cooperative parish.

7. Parish development aids (see Appendix C). This six-session course is designed for use by the committee composed of representatives from each church or institution. It is based upon the principles as outlined in this chapter and designed to help the committee do its work. The underlying principles are that the committee will: (a) Study the local region. Research is necessary. Chapter 8 of this book outlines the type of research needed and the process by which the research can be done. Persons are interested in statistics when they are a part of them. (b) Study the types of cooperative parishes. (c) Study the work of cooperative parishes. (d) Attempt to apply the knowledge gained to their own situation. (e) Be teachers within their own congregation or institution. In the formal

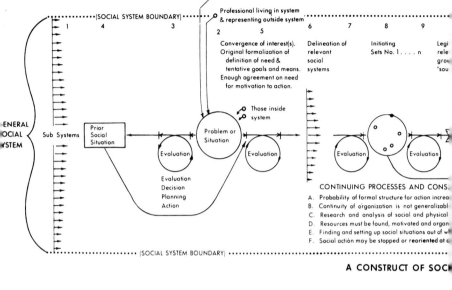

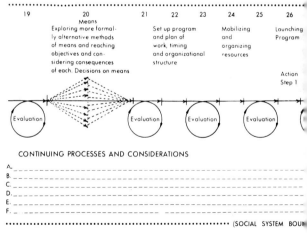

Figure 14.   A Construct of Social Action.

From George M. Beal, "Social Action: Instigated Social Change in Larg (Ames: Iowa State University Press, 1964). Both this chart and the ma article.

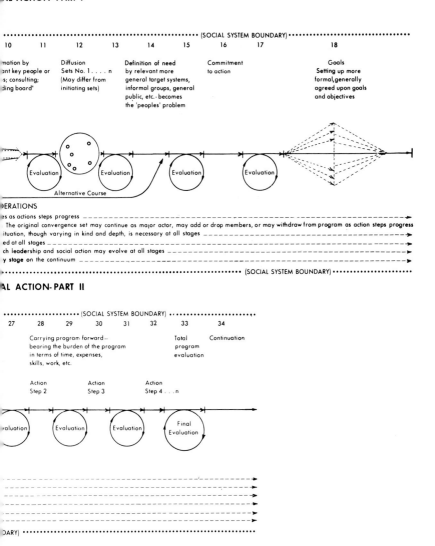

•• (SOCIAL SYSTEM BOUNDARY) ••••••••••••••••••••••••

| 10 | 11 | 12 | 13 | 14 | 15 | 16 | 17 | 18 |

mation by ont key people or s; consulting; ding board"

Diffusion Sets No. 1 . . . . n (May differ from initiating sets)

Definition of need by relevant more general target systems, informal groups, general public, etc.- becomes the 'peoples' problem

Commitment to action

Goals **Setting up more formal, generally agreed upon goals and objectives**

)ERATIONS

es as actions steps progress _____➤

The original convergence set may continue as major actor, may add or drop members, or may withdraw from program as action steps progress

ituation, though varying in kind and depth, is necessary at all stages _____➤

ed at all stages _____➤

ch leadership and social action may evolve at all stages _____➤

y stage on the continuum _____➤

•• (SOCIAL SYSTEM BOUNDARY) ••••••••••••••••••••••

•••••••••••••••••••• (SOCIAL SYSTEM BOUNDARY) ••••••••••••••••••••••••••••••

| 27 | 28 | 29 | 30 | 31 | 32 | 33 | 34 |

Carrying program forward— bearing the burden of the program in terms of time, expenses, skills, work, etc.

Total program evaluation

Continuation

Action Step 2

Action Step 3

Action Step 4 . . . n

valuation / Evaluation / Evaluation / Final Evaluation

)ARY) ••

e Social Systems," in James H. Coop, ed., *Our Changing Rural Society* erial describing the process of social action are adapted from Mr. Beal's

AN INFORMAL PROCESS FOR PARISH DEVELOPMENT

1.
Initiation

2.
Temporary geographic area

3.
Possible congregations and church institutions

4.
Meeting of pastors & key leaders

5.
Leaders discuss the possibilities with official church bodies

6.
Each body gives approval for exploration and elects representatives

Layman, pastor, executive

Locality group (see chs. 2 & 3)

Parish Development Aids (See Appendix C)

7.
Representatives from each church or institution meet to study, analyze, do research, examine needs, study ways of meeting needs, establish goals and objectives, and inform local churches and institutions

8.
Representatives diffuse information back to local churches and institutions and receive sanction to continue the study

9.
Repeat 7 & 8

10.
Repeat 7 & 8

11.
Repeat 7 & 8

12.
Repeat 7 & 8

13.
Repeat 7 & 8 Decision in study group for type of cooperative parish and submission of plan to local churches and institutions

14.
Each local church and institution will approve the plan, pledge support, and participation

15. ACTION

The cooperative parish

97

description of a construct for social action, item 12 is "Diffusion Sets." These are the persons who diffuse the information back in each congregation. After each meeting of the committee the representatives will share in their respective congregations or institutions what has taken place in committee discussion. It may be advisable for the official bodies to give a vote of approval for continued discussion. They can raise questions which will be brought back to the committee for clarification. They can stop the discussions if they feel it is not beneficial. (f) The committee after numerous meetings will make a decision as to the type of cooperative parish they feel will meet their needs. This is then shared with each local congregation and institution for approval.

"Parish Development Aids" is designed for a minimum of six sessions. These need to be spaced over a period of at least six months.

8-12. Continued meetings of the committee with appropriate feedback into the congregations and institutions.

13. Decision within the committee in regard to the type and program of the cooperative parish.

14. Decision by congregations and institutions. Each cooperating congregation and institution will, through the appropriate representative body (official board, administrative council, presbytery, deacons, etc.) or by congregational vote, approve the plan and pledge cooperation.

15. Action. Steps are then taken to get the organization into operation.

The plan is long and time-consuming. It will take from six months to as long as two years to work from the initial conception of the idea to the actual getting under way. It must be kept in mind we are dealing with groups of people who are not accustomed to radical institutional change. There will be the inevitable suspicions which must be overcome. There will be doubts. Usually some of the congregations have suffered defeat and seen their church slowly deteriorate. They have tried a number of programs only to see the church continue to be less effective. Many times the one word which will describe the general attitude is "discouraged."

It must also be admitted that frequently laymen are suspicious of pastors and especially of denominational executives. They may have felt there has been, in times past, the misrepresentation of truth or action which could not stand up under careful ethical examination. This may be an entirely unjust feeling, but when it is present it is a major barrier.

The community development process and the church-planning process have been formulated into a science. A detailed bibliography is given at the end of the book for further reading in the field.

VI

The Cooperative
Parish in Action

One of the basic theses of this work is—employed staff and organizations are for the purpose of assisting the layman to be the church in worship, nurture, and at work in the world. Therefore, the task of the cooperative parish is no different from that of a local congregation, but is designed to assist a local congregation to do a better job of being the church. One of the tragedies of the contemporary church is its limitation in areas of service within the world. Congregations become ingrown and self-satisfied without any feeling of a need for expansion in a greater fulfillment of the task of mission in the world. The cooperative parish offers many opportunities for creative means of witnessing to the Word in the world.

The Council

Cooperative parishes need to have a council composed of representatives from each congregation. The number of representatives will be determined by the size of the parish and number of congregations. Ordinarily, there are from one to three persons elected from each local congregation to serve on the parish council. The parish council becomes the major planning body for the activities of the total parish. The council will meet periodically to plan the total activities for the parish involved. Generally, once a month or each quarter is adequate, depending upon the size of the parish. The council needs to make serious studies of the needs within the local area. One of the valuable lessons taught by the inner city missions has been that the mission will start with the immediate needs of the people in the area. Frequently, the needs are for economic improvement and better health measures; thus, the parish begins by attempting to meet such physical needs. The program then expands to the development of the religious life of the people involved and eventually into a more crystallized form of church organization. In most of our nonmetropolitan areas, churches come together to form cooperative parishes, and the needs are primarily those of ministering within an existing congregation. The congregation then begins to examine the needs of the local area and take measures to minister to those needs.

The parish council will need subcommittees responsible for the various activities of the parish which are reflected through the work of local congregations. Most denominations have programs which center within six major areas: evangelism, mission, education, Christian social concern, worship, and stewardship. Some denominations may have as many as ten or twelve committees, and others may have less than the six major areas listed. Nevertheless, study has revealed that the six basic areas will cover almost every phase of activity and concern of a local church. Within the parish council, subcommittees should be established for each of the six basic areas, with responsibility for assisting local congregations and the parish at large in fulfilling the mission of the church. In addition, there will need to be subcommittees for women's work, men's work, and youth activities. The nine committees will generally be sufficient to meet the organizational needs of the parish.

The committees of the council need ample opportunity for reporting at various council meetings and also for bringing to the council in a detailed form the interest of the total parish within their field. Each committee should have authority to move into local congregations to assist in implementing their particular work area.

On occasion there will need to be special committees or task groups appointed to look after certain interests of the parish such as charge boundaries, church location and cooperation, farm and home interests, cooperation with community agencies, lay speakers, and special parish events.

The most active persons within each local congregation need to be elected to the parish council, and the strongest leadership of the parish should be the officers of the council.

The executive committee, usually consisting of the elected officers of the council, needs to meet on occasion with the employed staff of the cooperative parish to keep the coordinated program alive and effective. The members of the employed staff are ex officio members of the council and as such are to be present at each meeting and have the right of the floor and the vote. Strong lines of communication should be maintained at all times between the council, the employed staff, and each local congregation.

Financing the Cooperative Parish
in Nonmetropolitan Areas

The type of financial program for a cooperative parish is dependent upon the type of parish involved. If the parish consists of one rural community (locality group II), which is a town with its surrounding rural neighborhoods (locality group I), it is possible to have a completely unified budget. In this case the parish council will draw up a budget consisting of staff salaries, the denominational executive's salary, connectional items for the denomination or denominations, mission giving, and any other item which affects the total parish. Allowances need to be made for staff travel, office expense, the parish paper, and special parish events. Each church within the parish will accept its proportionate share of the budget and pay to a common treasurer, who in turn will make all payments for the parish. Each local congregation will need a treasurer who will receive funds from the members of the church through their regular contributions. He will make the payments for the congregation through the parish treasurer. Each local congregation will take care of its church school literature, building maintenance, custodial services, and utilities. The unified budget described above has been found to operate very successfully in many cooperative parishes. The unified budget will operate quite effectively in the extended ministry, enlarged charge, larger parish, or yoked field.

In the group ministry, support of individual staff members, with the exception of a specialized worker who serves the whole area, should come from the charge served by the individual pastor. Each pastor in the group ministry serves one or more congregations. This is his definite responsibility, and he should receive his salary from the churches he serves. In this event, the group ministry as such does not have a large central treasury. It will need to have a treasurer who will receive funds from each church to support enterprises involving all of the churches. Supported from the central fund are such items as a parish paper, office expenses for the director, an annual parish day, and other cooperative activities. If there is a specialist—such as a rural worker—who serves the total area, this person's salary and travel expenses should be paid through the common fund. The group ministry ordinarily is operated in the enlarged community (locality groups III and VI) where ties are not strong enough for a program of closely integrated operation, such as the larger parish.

Treasurers need to keep very accurate records of all receipts and disbursements, and books should be available for examination by any person or group within the parish. An annual audit needs to be made by impersonal auditors and a report made to the parish council. This should also be published in some kind of parish-wide circular.

The question is inevitably raised by laymen and church executives, "How much in outside funds is necessary to invest in a cooperative parish?" A second question is, "How long should outside funds be invested in a cooperative parish?" The answers to these questions are obviously relevant. Many cooperative parishes are started without any invested funds from denominational boards. Some groups require an investment for a stated period of time, while others may require support indefinitely.

Some general principles may be stated:

1. The territory for a cooperative parish needs to have sufficient resources for self-support under normal conditions. Frequently it is necessary to make an investment in staff support to "prime the pump." Many times good stewardship principles have not been instilled in the church members due primarily to poor ministerial leadership, or none. With good ministerial leadership, sound stewardship teaching, and good administrative policies the level of giving within local congregations can be increased.

Numerous studies have revealed a high correlation between increased church activities, effective ministerial leadership, increase in church school and church worship and increase in giving.

2. In most cases when outside support is supplied, it needs to be done on a specific time schedule and with diminishing amounts. Some boards of missions will allocate funds for a three-year period, decreasing the amount each year.

3. There are some situations in which the economic level is so low that there is a need for mission support for an indefinite time. If this is the case, boards of missions need to take this into consideration and expect to make a sustained allocation of funds for an indefinite period.

Financing the Cooperative Parish in Urban Areas

The group ministry or cluster group in the ordinary urban setting will need little support from denominational boards of missions. Each pastoral charge is a unit unto itself and is self-supporting. There may be a central treasury to support joint enterprises such as a parish newsletter, secretarial help, or a joint project. It is conceivable that as needs emerge for special types of ministries, larger sums of money will be needed.

The inner city parish is usually of a different nature. In this case there are old existing churches which have, in many situations, lost their major supporting members. These will be churches of minority racial, ethnic, or cultural groups with a membership in the lower economic levels. Almost without exception the inner city parish will need large sums of money from outside the parish. Funds will need to be supplied by denominational boards of missions on a local, regional, and national level. In most cases, there is not hope of the parish's getting to a self-supporting stage, which means boards of missions will need to gear their budgets to make continued contributions over a long period of time. Local congregations need to make contributions to the local church budget and the parish budget in as equitable manner as possible. Persons with low incomes can share in their church expenses, and need to for their own Christian stewardship witness.

Cooperative Activities of a Parish

There are many areas of cooperation involving all the churches within a parish. The ingenuity of the group in planning can discover areas that are beyond this discussion.

The parish paper. An essential in any kind of cooperative ministry is some type of parish paper, which can take the form of a mimeographed page or a rather elaborate, printed magazine-type of publication. Regardless of the actual form, there are several underlying principles which need to be observed:

1. The paper should not be on a subscription basis. Support should come from the cooperating churches on the basis of the number of families in the church. If there is no central treasury from which such a paper can be supported, it would need to be supported by the local churches involved. This support could come from an amount set aside in the church budget, from the church school, or from individual contributions. The paper will be defeated in its purpose if subscriptions are taken. Any subscription paper will not go to all families. The paper should also be mailed to all constituents of the church in the

parish as a means of cultivating prospects for parish membership. Support is not difficult to obtain after the paper has had two or three issues.

2. The paper needs to be mailed from one central office to all families within the membership of the churches of the parish. It needs to be mailed to all prospective families for church membership. Such a list of prospects can be compiled by careful examination of church school records, youth activity rolls, women's society rolls, and lists of persons contacted in any organization within the church. Additional members of families who are not members of the church will be discovered. Visitation cards should be carefully kept for persons visiting in church services. The community house-to-house survey is a source of discovering membership prospects. Any family contacted in any way by the church or any family without a church home becomes a potential for church membership. These persons need to receive the parish paper.

3. The paper needs to have a standing column which announces the church service schedule for all congregations, names and addresses of staff members, ministers, and members of the lay council.

4. The paper should carry articles of general concern to the entire area. It needs to be used as a means of announcing events involving all churches and reports of events which have taken place. A column needs to be devoted to the activities of each church, using the names of persons freely in reporting local church activities. Space should be given to denominational programs of general, churchwide nature. Many readers will not receive the church organ of the denomination, and the parish paper can provide a limited amount of general information. There needs to be a calendar of events and announcements. Articles on timely topics by members of the staff need to

be published, but sermons, generally, are not very interesting reading.

5. Someone within the parish—a minister, the director, or a layman—should be appointed by the council to be the editor of the paper. The best talent available needs to be secured for this task. It does take time, but it is one of the efforts that will pay large dividends when well done. The usual news formula of who, when, where, what, and why can be applied to preparing news articles. News is a reporting of incidents that people will find interesting.

6. The mechanics of preparing and distributing the paper must be assigned to some person or persons designated by the council. A good mimeograph production has the advantage of being more inexpensive than printing. Stress, however, should be placed on quality. Care needs to be taken preparing stencils, the use of the heavy paper, proper ink, and uniform distribution of ink. Contemporary offset types of printing will produce a nicer paper than mimeograph at a relatively inexpensive cost. Frequently a small town printer will prepare the paper in printed form for only a little more cost than mimeographing. Much more material can go into a printed paper than a mimeographed one. Sixteen pages of double-spaced typed material can be printed onto four sheets of the same size. Printing and offset have the added advantage of the use of pictures.

The person responsible for circulating the paper must have resources available for keeping an up-to-date mailing list. This needs to be revised constantly through the assistance of staff members. Some type of addressing machine should be supplied by the council. Mailing can be done under a special postal law regulation permit for nonprofit organizations, which provides mailing at a minimum cost per copy.

Activity groups in the parish. There are three main activity groups within the structure of the organized church: youth, men, and women. As far as possible, each of these groups needs to be recognized in planning the overall program of the cooperative parish. If the parish is denominational, the program of the denomination should be used. If interdenominational, the program can be designed to appeal to interests for the entire area and to stimulate a stronger program in the local church.

There should be a youth organization consisting of all young people from each local church. This cannot, except in the case of a very small parish, take the place of local church organizations. Young people enjoy the fellowship of other young people. They enjoy going places, and will go places when left on their own. A monthly parish meeting of the young people consisting of periods of worship, study, and recreation, will create interest and strengthen the entire Christian cause. Once each year the youth from all churches need to have a prolonged program covering the greater part of three days. Such a program can be in the winter; the young people can meet at the sponsoring church beginning with the evening meal on Friday, continue through Saturday, and close with the noon meal on Sunday. The program for such a meeting must be well balanced between worship opportunities, study classes on timely topics, and recreation. The sponsoring church can entertain the young people in homes overnight and through breakfast. Other meals can be provided by the women's society. A small fee can be charged to cover expenses. When church building facilities are not adequate, frequently the high school building can be used. The members of the parish staff can be used as speakers, teachers, and recreation leaders. The denominational personnel from connectional offices will be happy to give such leadership.

A strong program of summer camping ought to be promoted for youth in the parish. Young people can attend their denominational camps, but emphasis can be placed upon the camp by the entire group. The work of the men can be greatly enhanced by periodic meetings of all men from the cooperating churches. These meetings can be held at different churches at stated times. There should be some type of organization of the men, placing responsibility for program and planning in the hands of proper persons. Frequently the men's organization becomes the sponsoring agent for a laymen's speaking group to supplement worship services in the parish and to speak in local churches on timely subjects. Fellowship can be stimulated by a men's organization, creating splendid worship and learning opportunities.

The work of the women of the parish is usually more clearly defined by their denominational societies than the work of the men. Many small congregations, however, find the denominational organization too complicated to follow. It is difficult to have an active society with five women, when the organization calls for sixteen officers. Nevertheless, the five women need the fellowship and strength of the larger organization. Sometimes a small church can organize as a circle of a larger church not too far away. Certain activities can be done together, such as business and study sessions or special training classes. The stronger churches can be of great assistance to the smaller churches.

Leadership education. The cry from churches across the nation is constantly for more and better-trained church school leaders and teachers. The cooperative parish provides a means for training teachers and church leaders by having annually, or twice each year, training classes on a parish-wide basis. It is difficult to secure teachers for leadership classes for the very small congregation, but teachers can be secured for a leadership school in which there are a number of churches cooperating. Transportation facilities make it possible for teachers to travel to such training schools several miles away. Denominational executive secretaries of education will welcome the opportunity to assist in setting up schools and providing teachers. Classes should be conducted in administration of the church school; methods of teaching children, youth, and adults; how to use literature, the Bible, church history, theology; and many subjects relevant to the teaching-learning process.

The Parish Day. At least annually there should be a parish day, drawing all members of all congregations together for a full day of church activity. The program should be on Sunday and consist of church school for all age groups, morning worship service, a basket dinner, and an afternoon program. The observance would probably tax the capacity of the largest church building in the area and needs to be held in some type of open-air pavilion. A special lay council committee will be needed to make the plans. Such plans call for selecting church school teachers, selecting the speaker for the day, providing the facilities for the meeting—tables for the dinner, musical instruments, drinking water, rest rooms, parking grounds, hymn books, a printed order of service, the program, choirs, and persons to assist in parking cars. The speaker for the day will need to be a specialist in the field of town and country work, urban work, evangelism, or social action. His expenses—travel, entertainment, and an honorarium— can be provided for from the offering at the meeting.

The parish day brings a spirit of enthusiasm to the entire constituency. It gives the members of the individual churches an opportunity to meet others in the parish and gives the parish an opportunity to express its strength. Widespread publicity will be given to such a meeting by public press. The parish witnesses as a cooperative program for the Christian cause. It makes an opportunity to bring to the area outstanding national leadership in the field of town and country church or urban church, as the case may be. This is not possible for a church working alone, but when resources are pooled, leaders are anxious for the opportunity to participate in such a gathering.

Further Cooperative Parish Concerns

The usual urban group ministry or cluster group will operate in the same manner as a nonmetropolitan group ministry. Each pastor receives support from a local congregation or congregations. There will be some pooled resources for a parish paper and other joint activities. This can expand as needs are discovered which may be met by a joint undertaking such as a community house for a specific purpose of meeting human needs, a clinic, a recreation center, special ministry such as a halfway house, and so on.

All cooperative parishes, both rural and urban, need to be aware of, and cooperate with, government agencies. In addition to the agencies operating in both town and country, in the rural areas the various agricultural agencies can be of assistance. The conservation services, country agricultural agent, home demonstration agent, 4-H club leaders, and high school Future Farmers and Future Homemakers department can provide invaluable services.

Ordinarily the urban inner city parish has a closer relationship to various governmental agencies than the rural. Housing, employment, food programs, health pro-

112

grams, legal services, direct relief, all are related to the church programs of offering services to the needy.

A word of caution needs to be made. In the midst of meeting the physical needs, the church stands in the unique position of offering a ministry to the spiritual needs of people. Parish staffs and councils need to plan carefully to provide a ministry of worship, religious growth, counseling, and ministry in times of crisis. The usual pastoral services are essential. Time becomes a factor, and it is easy to neglect the pastoral ministries in the demands for direct physical ministries.

Specialized Ministries

The cooperative parish offers a unique possibility for varying types of specialized ministries. Only a few are mentioned here as suggestive. Each local parish needs to make a thorough analysis of needs within the area and should attempt to develop a ministry to meet the needs.

Radio ministry. Counseling centers for problems related to marriage, legal matters, drug abuse, alcoholics, housing, language studies, occupational adaptation, health or mental problems, financial resources, or other areas. Poverty and direct relief. Teaching occupational skills such as typing. Ministry to persons in leisure. Ministries in institutions such as homes for the aged, hospitals, mental institutions, penal institutions, schools. Recreational programs or centers. Day care for children. Nursery schools. Many other special needs will emerge as groups work together and analyze the needs of the community.

The Balanced Community

Parish councils in both rural and urban areas need to examine their community to determine if the needs of the area are being met. All persons stand in need of "life-support systems." These systems are directly related to individual and corporate human needs. If they are not supplied, then it becomes necessary for persons to migrate to an area where they can be supplied, or the persons will be deprived of some life essentials.

Following is a framework for parish councils and parish staffs to use as they examine the life-support systems within the cooperative parish area.

The life-support systems suggested for examination are economics, religion, education, health and welfare, legal services, communication, recreation and fine arts, and conservation. The diagram, Figure 16, attempts to illustrate the balance of a community which supplies the eight basic areas of services. I am indebted to William Stacy, Extension Sociologist for many years at Iowa State University of Science and Technology for the basic structure.

An attempt is made in this writing to offer a structure for examination by parish councils of their own community either rural or urban, and thus, to provide a basis for joint approach to meeting deficiencies. Parish councils can use the following or a similar directive to examine the various life-support systems of the area. The directive is suggestive rather than exhaustive. In each instance there will need to be a task force or special study committee established to examine the area. Recruitment of churches of other denominations and private and public agencies is important.

1. *Religion.* What is the religious profile of the community? How many churches are there, and where are they located? What is the participation within each church, e.g., membership, actual attendance at worhsip, and other activities? What is the religious education program of each church? What are the social outreach services provided in each? From where does each church draw its member-

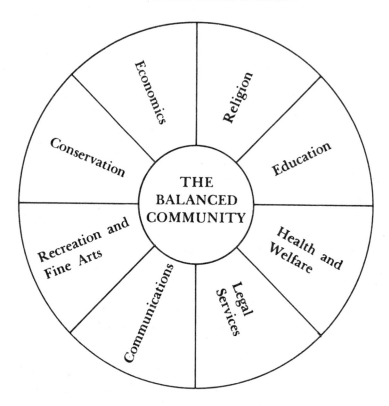

Figure 16. The balanced community in which the eight major life-support systems are available.

ship? (Many times in older urban congregations in areas of transition, the larger number of members live outside of the immediate vicinity of the church.) Who are the un-churched? (An actual survey may be necessary to get full information. A spot survey may be sufficient, that is, a sample of every fourth or fifth house.) What needs to be done to make available more meaningful religious op-portunities? How can this best be done? Who will accept the responsibility?

2. *Education.* What is the educational level of the community? (This can be obtained from U.S. Census reports.) Where are the public and private elementary and high schools located? What are their enrollments? Are they increasing or decreasing? Are the educational needs of exceptional children being met—the brilliant as well as the slow learner? Are the facilities adequate? What is the relationship between the parents of children in school and the school administrators and faculty? Are there inequities in the school with racial or minority groups? How many young people are in college? Is there a need to assist more youth in considering college? Is there a need for more and better vocational training? Are the needs for preschool children being met? What adult education needs are there? Are they being met? How can they be more adequately met? What can the churches of the cooperative parish do to assist in improving the education needs of the community?

3. *Economic.* What is the economic level of the community? Are there job opportunities for persons of different age levels? Many towns cannot supply the job opportunities for young people completing their schooling, making it necessary for youth to migrate to other areas. Is there a need to stimulate the beginning of new industries in the area? Is there a need to assist in developing father-son operating agreements in farm or business operations?

Is there a large segment of the poor? Are their needs being met? What is the housing situation? Is there a need to lift the level of housing quality? What civic and government agencies are at work on the economic needs of the community? How can the church stimulate more action in the economic needs of people in the community? Who will do the work?

4. *Health and welfare.* What is the health situation in

116

the community? Is there a high rate of communicable disease? What is being done about the health problems? Are there adequate hospital facilties? Are there enough doctors available? Is there a need for clinic space to be provided by a church or churches? Are there persons in the community who cannot receive adequate medical treatment due to a lack of income or health insurance? Do persons need transportation to and from the health centers? Are there problems in relation to drugs or alcohol? What is being done, and what can the churches in the community do, to assist in raising the health level of the community? Who will do it?

5. *Legal services.* Is the municipal government providing adequate services in the community? Is there good and fair police protection? Is there a need to establish a counseling service for persons in regard to legal rights? What other agencies in the community are attempting to improve legal services and how can the cooperative parish work with the agency?

6. *Communication.* What are the conditions of the roads or streets in the area of the cooperative parish? Is there discrimination in road or street construction or maintenance due to economic levels? What are the newspapers in the area? Is their reporting fair to all interests of the community? Is there a need to suggest different editorial policies? What are the radio and television stations in the area? Is it possible to receive more coverage for religious, educational, and cultural programming?

7. *Recreation and cultural arts.* Are there adequate recreational facilities of an acceptable cultural and moral level in the region for persons in different age levels? Is there need for the churches, schools, and civic organizations to work together to develop better recreational facilities? Are there recreational centers in the area, such

as lakes, rivers, mountains, which attract persons in leisure and for which the church needs to be providing some type of ministry? What organizations in the region are attempting a meaningful program of recreation to children, youth, or adults? What is their program, and can the church be of assistance in it? Are there adequate programs for assisting persons in retirement to a meaningful use of time?

8. *Conservation.* What are the needs for a meaningful conservation program in the area? Are there problems of pollution of air, water, and natural resources? What needs to be done to preserve the natural beauty and resources of the area? What agencies are engaged in conservation programs in the area, and how can the church be of assistance to such agencies?

Denominational Policies

One of the problems cooperative parishes have faced is the continued interest and moral support of the denomination or denominations involved. There is a decided need for denominational judicatorial bodies to prepare policy statements which will protect the cooperative parish over a long period of time.

Policies need to be clear in regard to the cooperative parish plan's being a normal part of the denomination's system. In the episcopal appointive system leaders will need to inform a minister or ministers going to a parish of what is to be expected. The appointee must be willing to accept the responsibility for the parish as a part of his or her work. Salary must be understood to be based upon the total amount from each church.

If the parish is interdenominational ministers need to be assured of full rights of appointment or call by the cooperating denominations. There needs to be an understood participation by the clergy in the governing bodies of the denominations. Retirement annuities need to be worked out. Such policies need to be worked through on the judicatory level and adopted by the governing body.

VII

Leadership
and Human Relations

As congregations, ministers, and lay employees with professional skills unite their resources to work together in cooperative parishes, the matter of leadership and human relations will need to be given much attention. Education for ministry in theological seminaries all too often does not include much training in personnel management and leadership skills. It becomes essential for staffs in cooperative parishes to spend much time in study of staff relations. Staffs need to work toward aspects of developing procedural practices which will make for efficient work and maximize the talents of all involved. The "distances" between staff members are usually quite large. Some common areas of distance are: range in amount and type of education, theological concepts, perceptions of the involvement of the leaders in social action, concepts of worship, denominational traditions, and ethnic, racial, and nationality backgrounds. Each person brings to the cooperative parish staff a self-image and personal goals and objectives. At some point these goals and objectives need to converge into agreed-upon goals and objectives for the cooperative parish.

In addition to employed staff, there are a number of involved leaders and groups within the parish. Each local congregation will have a number of subgroups organized. Each has leaders. The denomination or denominations involved will have executives who will be a part of the leadership. When funds are supplied by a denominational board or agency, the agency representatives will want to be considered in the administration of the parish. It does not take much imagination to visualize the aspects of human relations that need to be considered in a cooperative parish.[1]

Basic aspects of human relations within the parish staff are discussed in this chapter. Principles of personnel management are suggested which are designed to assist the staff in developing their skills of working together.

Staff Considerations

1. *Salary arrangements.* Fair pay is far more important than just good pay. Employment satisfaction is dependent upon whether or not the employee feels he has been treated fairly in the light of peers in the same general age and position brackets. Church officials need to study salary arrangements for persons in similar positions, persons with similar education and experience, and persons with comparable positions in rural and urban employment.

Salaries for all members of the staff should be examined in the light of responsibilities, age, experience, and family responsibilities. Too large a salary differential in a staff can be grounds for much unhappiness. Some staffs solve the problem by establishing an equal salary base with compensation for family size.

121

2. *Housing.* It is customary within Christendom to supply housing for the minister. This is recognized by the federal government in that house rent and monetary housing allowance are nontaxable. Fairly equal housing needs to be provided for all members of the staff. The customs of the denominations cooperating should be taken into account.

3. *Retirement plans.* All members of the staff need to be provided with some type of retirement plan. Most denominations have retirement plans for ordained clergy. The unordained member of the staff, however, is often forgotten. Most denominations usually have some plan whereby unordained church employees can come under their retirement plan. It is necessary for a local church to apply for the plan. Social Security is now available for all nonordained employees on the institutional-share basis. Ordained clergy, however, must carry their own Social Security as self-employed.

4. *Travel.* All persons employed must have an adequate travel allowance. The demands for pastoral services require much travel. Parish councils or official boards should make a fair allowance for travel. One parish staff is allowed five hundred dollars a year per staff person "for the car" and an additional six cents per mile. The five hundred dollars is for insurance and a "nest egg" to purchase the next car. The six cents per mile is for fuel and upkeep. The staff members are quite happy with the arrangement.

5. *A system of salary advancement.* Some system of regular increases in salaries needs to be established. Advancements should be made on the basis of experience, years of service, and the general economic trend.

6. *Stated vacation and leave time.* Each member of the staff needs to be given an annual vacation with pay. This will vary with denominations and customs. Some

form of sabbatical leave needs to be established so that an extended time every three to six years can be arranged, giving staff members three to six months for travel or study.

All of the above arrangements need to be put in writing by the parish council or official board. Much misunderstanding can be avoided if the above suggestions are adhered to.[2]

7. *A job description.* A job description is a written statement which defines areas of work and responsibilities. There needs to be a job description for each employed member of the staff. Basically the job description assists the individual in understanding his own position and his relationship with other employed members of the staff. It helps the congregation or cooperating congregations to understand the duties, functions, and responsibilities of the members of the staff. A job description should be reviewed every six months to a year in a new organization and revised as needs arise. It should be considered as a descriptive, rather than as a legally binding, document.

The job description needs to contain the following elements: (*a*) statement of title of positions; (*b*) lines of responsibility, e.g., to whom the party is responsible for reporting, advice, guidance, complaints, or requests; (*c*) a statement of duties and responsibilities; (*d*) a schedule (flexible) of work time; (*e*) vacation periods, days off, and holidays to be observed; (*f*) salary, retirement benefits, expense accounts, and other considerations; (*g*) opportunities for self-improvement; and (*h*) advancements.[3]

In a cooperative parish the congregations should be informed through a brief, concise publication about the members of the staff and the responsibilities of each person on the staff. The people need to know to whom they can look for their pastoral needs, who will be conducting ser-

123

vices of worship in their church, and who is responsible for the various activities of the parish. Much confusion can be avoided if good job descriptions are prepared and followed.[4]

8. *The staff meetings.* Regular meetings of the employed staff are essential to develop an esprit de corps and to coordinate work. In any situation when two or more persons are jointly employed in related work a structured form of human relations associations is essential. There are four types of staff experience which are suggested to develop the type of working relationship needed in a parish staff: (*a*) worship, (*b*) fellowship, (*c*) business, and (*d*) study and personal enrichment. These are listed in the order of their priority.

Worship is placed first. Worship is at the heart of the Christian community and needs to be at the heart of the parish staff. Regular times of worship need to be provided; as far as possible, the worship needs to include spouses and children of the staff families. Worship may be simple or elaborate, but it does need to be planned, scheduled, and adhered to. Leadership needs to be shared by all persons in the staff.

Fellowship within the staff families is placed second in importance. Fellowship, along with worship is the basis of developing community, and out of it will grow understanding, love, and a sense of oneness in task and purpose. At least monthly the staff, including all members of the families, needs to get together for a covered-dish meal and fellowship. One of the most repeated complaints which is heard from ministers and their families is that their task is a lonely one. They feel the need for support from their peers. The cooperative staff provides a framework for such support. Spouses of staff members are an integral part of the leadership of a cooperative parish and need to be a part of the fellowship, and to a degree, engaged in planning the work.

Differences among the staff members and spouses in education, cultural background, and theological positions are minimized around the fellowship table. Jesus was using good psychology in developing a oneness among such a diverse group as his disciples when they frequently broke bread together.

The *business session* needs to be regularly scheduled. If the parish is a closely integrated type with a joint staff serving all the congregations and organizations involved, the meetings need to be once a week. If the cooperative parish is a group ministry or similar organization, once a month may be frequent enough for the meetings.

The meetings need to be well planned built around an agenda which has been provided by staff members and the interests of the parish.

Many staffs will engage in a staff retreat once or twice a year for a two-or three-day session. Such sessions are held in a campsite, retreat center, or a motel, and will usually include the families of staff members. Lay leadership in the parish may also be included.

The fourth type of meeting held by the staff is for *study and personal enrichment*. Academic fields related to the ministry are changing so rapidly and so much new literature is being produced that it is difficult to keep abreast of current thought. Stated times for staff study need to be set aside. This may involve a staff sharing of the exciting areas of reading each person has discovered. It may mean that periodically the staff will need to set aside one day a week for a period of six weeks to study an agreed upon subject— Christian ethies, church history, Bible, theology, or related fields. Continuing education programs provided by seminaries now facilitate structuring such studies.[5]

Relationships with Leadership Groups

A leadership group is any group within the parish which has leadership responsibility. Three main groups exist wthin most cooperative staff structures: (1) the employed staff; (2) the parish council; and (3) the official board of each congregation. Each of the above groups needs to possess a sense of autonomy, but at the heart of the work of each group is cooperation with every other group.

1. *The employed staff.* Parish staffs are in a position to direct the work of the parish, but at all times they should keep in mind that they are the servants of the congregation. The church is the laity, and the task of the staff is to help the laity be the church! Too often members of the staff become over-anxious and over-zealous in their desire to see the work of the parish develop and move ahead of the laity instead of developing lay leadership.

2. *The council.* In a cooperative parish there should be a council composed of representatives from each congregation. The members of the staff are ex officio members of the council. The primary purpose of the council is to be the initiator and promoter of the total program of the parish. In some situations the council will be responsible for selecting and employing staff.

The members of the council need to take their work seriously. They represent their local congregation and should at all times be in a position to take back to the local congregation the plans of the staff council and the parish staff, and to express personal opinions in group meetings and speak for the church. The council must be creative in thinking with the other members and the staff in developing a program for the group of churches in cooperation. Harmony will prevail if each member will do his work with sincerity to the best of his ability.

126

The chairman of the council is the presiding officer at all meetings. He should have a carefully prepared agenda and keep the business sessions moving orderly and on schedule. At all times the chairman needs to be in close touch with the director of the parish and members of the staff.

Numerous committees should be appointed within the staff. Ample opportunity needs to be provided in council meetings for committee reports.

3. *The official board.* (The term is used to represent the official body of a local church such as board of deacons, elders, presbyters, administrative board, or whatever applies in the particular denomination.) The purpose of a cooperative parish is to strengthen individual persons in each congregation. In other words, one of the major tasks of the cooperative parish is to assist each local congregation to be a better witness within its own membership and to the world. The official board should assist the congregation in being loyal to the parish program. If there is a constitution in the parish, it should be reviewed periodically. Official boards need to assist the congregation in interpreting the constitution and to bear the sentiments of the congregation to the parish council. Representatives from the local congregation on the parish council must have ample opportunity to report the actions of the council in board meetings. Dates for council activities should be cleared, proposed programs presented, reports of parish activities made. At times the board must report to the congregation in Sunday church school and services of worship with regard to the work of the parish. It is essential that clear channels of communication be maintained between council, the parish staff, the official board, and the congregation. The official board can serve as a liaison between these groups.

A fourth position of leadership needs to be kept in mind.

That is the *denominational executive official*. Most denominations have field representatives who are assigned to a geographic region and who are responsibile for assisting the congregations in the region. The area may be known as a synod, district, county, state, or other region. The work of the executive may vary greatly from purely advisory to administrative. In every case, however, the denominational representative is a valuable person to assist in establishing and maintaining cooperative parishes. On occasion he may be able to provide the basic research necessary in the early stages of a parish and may be in a position to inform congregations of the meaning of a parish and advantages which will come from the organization. Many times the denominational representative can be the person who brings a cooperative parish into existence. He is the professional assistant who can direct the entire organizational process.

It is often the denominational representative to whom the council will turn for suggestions regarding the staff. He is responsible for maintaining top quality leadership in the parish, and must assist the parish when a change of leadership is necessary. He is the liaison person between the parish, parish leadership, and the denominational connectional organization.

Some Qualification of a Director
of a Cooperative Parish

The success of failure of a cooperative program is dependent, to a large degree, upon the qualifications of the director for his position. A director's role is not easy. He or she must have the ability to lead others without the authority of a superior office; he or she must have a sufficient understanding of human nature to cope with the differences of personality characteristics, educational qualifications, theological prejudices and interpretations, and the psychological makeup of individuals in the staff.

Leadership qualifications for parish directors are the same for persons in town and country and urban areas, but the areas of awareness will differ. A brief summary is presented below.

Areas of awareness for a director of a parish in town and country are: (1) an appreciation of rural life, (2) a consecration to the task of service in the rural church, and (3) a knowledge or rural social systems and rural sociology.

1. *An appreciation of rural life.* A director must be in sympathy with rural life, feeling that there is a definite contribution rural people make to the total culture. One of the basic theories of sociology is that there is always a tendency for urban culture to dominate the total thinking of a people and that rural life is minimized in importance. This is reflected in the fact that there is always a migration of population from rural to urban areas except in time of catastrophe, such as war or famine. The bright lights of the city attract the attention of the nation. There is a premium placed upon the professional man who makes a success of his work in the city—doctor, lawyer, teacher, minister. One who does a successful work in a rural area is seldom recognized until he has had the stamp of approval placed upon him by the city. A parish director must be mindful of these facts. He must be willing to work in the framework of this knowledge, accepting the role for the merits in the case. These merits are legion. The parish director must feel his task is important in the whole economy of the nation, important in his denomination, and in the universal church.

If a director regards the position as a steppingstone to a better position or one more prominent in his church, he

129

had better refuse it. He should feel that this task is one of the most important positions in the church.

2. Closely related to the sense of appreciation of rural life is that of a *consecration to the task of service in the rural church.* With a shortage of qualified ministerial leadership in most of the leading denominations of the nation and the glamour of a rapidly growing urban culture with all the opportunities for the establishment of new churches, it is easy for one to lose his sense of mission to rural America. The Protestant churches do not recognize the rural pastorate in equal proporation to the urban, or even in equal proportion to the missionary who serves in a faraway land. There is the feeling that the minister who remains in a pastorate of leadership in the rural church somehow could not prove himself a capable leader for a larger responsibility. This is a phenomenon with which a parish director must reckon. He must be willing to face this situation, knowing full well certain recognitions will probably never come his way which do come to some ministers in his denomination. A sense of mission, a sense of calling, however, has always marked the prophet; and he has been willing, without complaint or defensiveness, to continue his work in the light of a task to be done. The director must live in a constant state of consecration—as should all ministers for that matter—holding the basic elements of the gospel ministry uppermost in his mind. It is helpful to keep in one's thinking the statements of Christ: "Even the Son of man came not to be ministered unto, but to minister"; "The servant is not greater than his lord"; "He that is greatest among you shall be your servant."

3. *A knowledge of rural social systems and rural sociology* is important to the parish director. There was a time when it was felt that a rural minister should be well versed in

agriculture so that he could, to a certain degree, serve as an agricultural consultant. In a day of specialization, when there are from one to ten full-time employed agricultural specialists in most counties in America and when theological training is a long and tedious process, the minister does not have time to train in agriculture, nor is there the need for it. He needs, however, to have enough training in modern agricultural methods to appreciate them and to guide the farmer within his parish to the specialist within his county. He needs to know how to work with the agricultural extension agent, the vocational agricultural teacher, the soil conservationist. He ought to be acquainted with the services available from the agricultural college within the state. His parish can be a means of contact for various social and agricultural agencies. This means the director must know the people who are working in his county and must have a close working relationship with them. He can be a member of farmer's organizations in the area, provided he can agree with their policies. They can be of assistance to his people, and he can be of assistance to them.

The director should have enough work in rural sociology and rural church administration to understand something of the nature of rural society. This will facilitate his getting along with people and his appreciation of the unseen forces which influence the minds of rural people. Group solidarity, intimacy of kin, clannishness, slowness in acceptance of new ideas, a reverence of tradition—all are marks of rural culture. The parish leader will recognize these and adjust his work to fit them rather than oppose them. If a director has not had the opportunity to study rural sociology formally, he should arrange for some short courses, additional seminary work, or courses in a department of sociology in a college or university. Constant reading in the field assists in keeping one abreast of scholarly developments.

Areas of awareness for a director of a parish in the city consist of: (1) an appreciation of the place of the church in urban America, (2) a consecration to the task of service in the urban setting, and (3) a knowledge of urban social systems and urban sociology.

1. *An appreciation of the place of the church in urban America.* It is essential that a parish leader feel strongly that the work of the church in essential and vital in urban America. He needs an appreciation of urban life with an awareness of the needs of people who make up the city. The needs of persons can become a challenge for an effective ministry.

2. *A consecration to the task of service in the urban setting.* Many urban parishes provide a setting in which the average minister is quite satisfied to live and rear a family. Other parishes, however, require the minister and family to live in an area of socio-cultural life which is not in keeping with their ideals. This can quickly throw a family into frustration and discontent. This is especially true with inner city parishes. Unless a family is able to identify with the people in their ministry by living in the same area, there may be a built-in blockage to an effective ministry. Families need to work through together the aspects of ministry which involve the family and attempt a consensus of opinion and agreement in dedication to the task.

3. *A knowledge of urban social systems and urban sociology* is essential for a parish leader in urban areas. The leader needs to be schooled in the process of urbanization, the dynamics of urban growth, the problems of population movements in centralization, decentralization, segregation, invasion, and succession. The leader needs to be thoroughly acquainted with the politics of the city. He needs

to know of agencies, both private and governmental, that are available to assist in a more effective ministry, and how one goes about communicating with the agencies. The leader will need to keep constantly alert to new movements, trends, research, and knowledge in urban social systems.

The Parish Leader as Administrator

The director must be able to get along with people. In the church there are a few situations in which a minister is in authority over another minister. In the episcopal form of government, certain officials—district superintendents and bishops—are delegated such authoritative positions, but a minister, though he may be a parish director, is still a minister among many. For this reason, the parish director must understand fully democratic leadership methods. He must be capable of throwing himself fully into the democratic process of group procedure, realizing that true democracy in group action is the most permanent form of group control. He must be winsome in personality, sincere in his motives, and have the ability to share with the ministers in the parish successes and failures. Precept and example are the best rules to follow. A task well done in his own responsibilities will speak loudly to the other ministers on the staff. A fellowship of the ministers, which emerges through informal group gatherings, frequent family dinners, occasional parties and picnics, will go a long way in breaking down any barriers between members of the staff.

One of the problems faced in a parish staff is the diversity in training of the ministers. Because of a shortage of ministers in many denominations, hundreds of men and women are being used as pastors who have not had the advantage

133

of formal education for the ministry. There is a tendency on the part of the untrained to hold rather dogmatic ideas on theological beliefs—which are defended with great emotion—and to feel that the trained person has lost his passion for the gospel. This makes for a decided barrier between the director and some members of the staff. Such barriers can be overcome with profound appreciation on the part of the director for the untrained minister who, in his own right, has a genuine call to the Christian ministry and a sincere desire to serve the church. Humility on the part of the director, appreciation for others, and a recognition of the contribution every person on the staff can make to the thinking of the group will aid in overcoming barriers of difference in education. Too much cannot be said regarding the necessity for a director to be brotherly, sincere, and honest in every respect in his work with the members of the staff.

Equally as difficult as the problems that arise with the untrained minister are the problems that may arise with the newly graduated seminarian. Frequently the young minister is assigned or elected to a position in a cooperative parish without understanding the nature of the work or the fundamental principles of cooperation. He can be quite vocal in his rejection of status quo theological positions of older staff members and outspoken against the existing church structures. He, like all persons entering into a cooperative ministry, needs to understand the nature of the assignment and should make a definite commitment to participation within the work. Murray H. Leiffer in *Changing Expectations and Ethics in the Professional Ministry* has made an excellent analysis of attitudes toward theology, ethics, and church authority on the basis of age and various positions in church leadership.[6]

The professional worker (often a woman) who is assinged to a cooperative parish has a difficult place to fill. Some denominations have trained workers who are specialists in community action and are assigned by the denomination to the position, and sometimes a specialist will be assigned or elected for work in Christian education within a cooperative parish. The most frequent problems which have occurred with the professional worker are lack of a clear-cut job description, lack of understanding of lines of authority, failure to understand the fundamentals of staff relationships and how to work with others, and lack of understanding of cultural patterns of the area in which the work is being done. Obviously there are many professional workers who have little difficulty in adjusting to staff work, but many do have problems. Frankness on the part of all persons on the staff in working through human relations will be beneficial.

The basic *distances* between members of a cooperative staff which need to be overcome are in age, theology, concept of the church, concept of the cooperative parish, education, cultural background, denominational background, and concepts of ethics and morality.

The alert parish director, along with the entire staff, will take time to understand differences and attempt to create situations in which differences will be minimized in favor of points of mutual concerns. Differences are not so important as long as communication is maintained and there are open minds. All persons on the staff need to develop a listening habit to hear other members of the staff and to have respect for their positions. Frequent discussion, fellowship situations, parties, and informal gatherings, assist greatly in coming to know the whole person rather than just the categories in which there are disagreements. One staff in the author's acquaintance, in which all of the above distances are present, has a Monday morning meeting on a riverbank in a sixteen-foot mobile home and finds this tremendous therapy. All staffs cannot enjoy this luxury, but they can create situations which will fulfill the same need.

All members of a cooperative staff need to have a working knowledge in the field of human relations. Time could be well spent if the staff would study together in the field. George R. Terry defines human relations: "Stated succinctly, by human relations is meant the integration of the manpower resources for effective and maximum utilization by means of satisfying human wants and the maintaining of satisfactory relationships among the members seeing those human wants." [7]

Each person will bring into a parish staff a hope of being able to satisfy his own personal wants and to make a contribution to the mutual concerns of the total staff. Basically the personal wants can be summarized as: (1) an opportunity for self-expression; (2) an opportunity to be recognized as an individual; (3) an opportunity to be accepted by the other members of the staff; (4) an opportunity to have a fair and equitable work load along with other members of the staff and to share a fair amount of pay and other remunerations; (5) acceptable working conditions; and (6) efficient leadership.

Those who are endowed with leadership responsibilities in a staff, such as the director, will expect from each member of the staff dependability, loyalty, creativeness, resourcefulness, cooperation, honesty, and a reasonable quantity of work well done.[8]

If a staff of a cooperative ministry is to attain the highest efficiency, each member should bring into accord with the other members his personal desires and goals of life, the desires of the leadership of the parish, and the parish objectives. Again it is stated that parish goals and ob-

LEADERSHIP AND HUMAN RELATIONS

jectives need to be clearly defined. As they are defined, persons on the staff will need to bring their own talents to bear upon attaining the goals. When a "we" feeling emerges in team ministry, the staff will begin to attain the proper perspective of group accomplishment.

Leadership Authority

One of the most vexing problems of staff relationships in a cooperative parish is that of authority for action and responsibility for the leader. I have encountered two major problems in cooperative parishes: either the director was elected or appointed to the position, but had no authority for administrative leadership; *or,* the director did not understand basic leadership principles and misused his authority, causing estrangement from other members of the staff.

Authority in the management sense, as defined by literature in personnel management, means power which is placed in a leader giving him the right to initiate, act, and exact action out of others. Along with this definition is the basic concept that authority needs to be invested in a leader commensurate with his responsibility. The reverse of this is also true. In other words, when a director of a cooperative parish is elected or appointed to the position, he is automatically held responsible for action and results. He must be granted the authority to act and to lead in order that such expected results can be forthcoming. In the atmosphere of democratic action, a council of a cooperative parish or denominational executive may be afraid of granting too much authority to a director for fear he will not be fair to other members of the staff. This only leads to frustration on the part of all staff persons and inevitable failure of the cooperative enterprise.

Freedom for action comes through sturctured authority.
It is highly recommended that when a cooperative parish is
established, involving an employed staff, a director be
elected or appointed and granted enough authority to be
able to initiate, act, and help each person on the staff make
a full contribution to the entire enterprise. In an episcopal
form of church government the appointment needs to be
made by the bishop.

In some instances the leader is elected by the group for
a stated period of time, and then another person is elected
as leader. A team concept is held by the staff, and the leader
becomes a convenor and moderator of staff meetings.
There are problems with such an arrangement, but it may
have merit, provided all members of the staff are near the
same age and have equal education and leadership ability.

Misused authority is the beginning of staff decay. Leaders need to study the democratic principles of leadership
and to understand the proper use of their position. Authority is automatically granted to a leader by the office he
holds, but support in authority is gained from one's peers
through an earning process. One is effective as a leader and
will gain support for his leadership when he has proved
personal integrity, honesty, sincerity, ability to produce in
his own field, and a genuine support of the total enterprise. When any one of these qualities is missing and a
doubt is forthcoming in the minds of staff members, then
there is trouble ahead.

A good leader never uses the power of his office with
overt authority. He is skillful in creating a situation in
which group decisions are made and the abilities of staff
are utilized to meet the needs of the parish. He will constantly keep in mind the personal desires of individuals
on the staff and attempt to keep lines of communication
open so all persons can obtain maximum of fulfillment.

Denominational Obligations

Every denomination has polity procedures in regard to placement of ministers. One of the most important aspects of polity is the adaptation by a denomination, or adoption by a regional governing body, of policies in regard to cooperative parishes. Three major areas of polity need to be considered: (1) qualifications of persons assigned or elected to parish staffs; (2) protection of the position in the staff when changes are made; and (3) a complete description of the position and statement of expected participation for the person being assigned to a cooperative parish. When any one of these three aspects is ignored, a foundation is laid for potential trouble. A brief discussion of the three points follows:

1. In assigning a person to a cooperative parish, care should be taken that the person has the necessary qualifications for the position. Something has been said about this earlier in this chapter. A loner will have difficulty working with others. Also a person who is overly dominant will have difficulties. A person who may have a negative attitude toward the church in town and country may feel he is being punished or degraded in his work. Every effort needs to be made to select persons who feel they are being challenged by the opportunity before them and that the task is one that will give ample expression to one's ministry.

2. Changes are necessary from time to time in the staff of a cooperative parish. When changes are made, the parish council and the denominational authorities need to take precaution that leadership is put into the parish which will continue the program. A person should not be appointed simply to take care of a situation, but care should be taken in the selection, with the type of leadership needed kept in mind.

3. Any person who is elected or appointed to a parish staff needs to have a complete briefing of the situation before he gets into the work. He needs to be informed of the nature of the work, lines of authority, his responsibilities, and his role in the staff. This is an area in which job descriptions are helpful. I visited in a larger parish where one minister was appointed to serve along with two other ministers. The superintendent had not explained the parish structure thoroughly and had failed to say there was a director of the parish already appointed. Naturally there are problems for the minister who comes into the parish with one idea and finds a different existing situation.

In closing this chapter, I add the thought that as long as there is human will, there will be conflicts of wills when people are engaged in a close working relationship. The task of a parish staff is to minimize conflict as much as possible by practicing democratic action, give-and-take, charity, and, above all, by each person's carrying his share of the load of work. The parish staff which finds time to fellowship together, plan together, work together, and worship together with an understood goal and objective will most likely find individual and corporate success in their work.

VIII

Research in Preparation
for a Cooperative Parish

The establishment of any type of a cooperative program should be preceded by sound research and survey. One of the pitfalls of larger parishes and group ministries has been the failure of leaders to recognize the natural forces of population, social groups, topography of the land, and economic factors, as they establish parishes. Brunner, for instance, in his 1933 study of the larger parish, realized parishes must have two physical factors to survive: (1) They must be a natural sociological unit, that is, a community; and (2) they must have sufficient economic resources to support themselves in normal times.[1] To these criteria could be added other factors such as a sufficiently large number of Protestant prospects to make the churches adequate to support a program, a spirit of cooperation between congregations and ministers, a willingness of the people to pool financial and leadership resources, the unreserved support of the central church, and a population which shows signs of enough stability for continued progress.

Not infrequently church leaders have plunged into a parish organization without sufficient knowledge of the ecological factors of the life of the population, only to find an organizationally impossible situation facing the parish. Time, energy, and disappointment will be saved when one does comprehensive research in preparation for the parish. Research findings when presented in graphic and tabular form will assist the people of a local area in understanding more fully their need for a cooperative undertaking by the churches.

The research does not need to be exhaustive, nor does it need to be done by a specialist. Nevertheless, if special help is available from a denominational executive, professor of sociology, or a professor of church administration, such help should be used. It is possible, in some situations, for a study to be done by a student or a group of students as a project in a college or seminary course.

The basic items for research are presented in this chapter. A sample questionnaire to be used by the local congregations is presented in Appendix B. Additional helps are suggested in the Bibliography.

Delineation of Neighborhood and Community in Nonmetropolitan Areas

The basic essential of a closely integrated larger parish, yoked field, enlarged charge, or extended ministry, interdenominational or denominational, is confinement to one community. A loosely integrated larger parish or group ministry can function efficiently if it embraces two or more rural communities, provided they are part of an enlarged community. The definitions of these meaningful sociological units (as given in chs. 2 and 3) are reviewed to refresh them in the mind of the reader. A community consists of the social interaction of people and their institutions in the local area in which they live on dispersed farmsteads and in a hamlet or village which forms the center of their common interests. An enlarged community is two or more communities bound together in a natural or political area with a dominant town in which all communities find a common interest. A review of chapters 2 and 3 will assist in understanding these basic structural units.

In establishing a closely integrated larger parish, the delineation of the community is necessary, and the boundaries of the parish should not go beyond the community. People will work together intimately in a community. They are accustomed to face-to-face relationships in school, church, trade, and social activities. They will not work closely together beyond community lines. Within a closely integrated larger parish there is one budget for several churches and two or more employed workers serving the entire parish. The parish council must serve as one board to direct the work of the parish, and the churches must have affinities sufficiently strong to override suspicion and friction. The same principle holds true for the yoked field, enlarged charge, or extended ministry.

In the loosely integrated larger parish or group ministry, each minister serves one or more congregations and derives his support from his charge. The parish council is not concerned with dispensing salaries to ministers. It assists the work of the local church but is not an official board in the administrative sense that it is for the closely integrated parish. Therefore, the loosely integrated parish or group ministry can cover more than one community. When it does, it should not go beyond one enlarged community. In the enlarged community there is one dominant town such as the county seat or leading trade center and two or more subdominant towns. A subdominant town is smaller in population and is able to offer fewer services than the dominant town. There are enough ties between the people of an enlarged community to warrant a loosely organized cooperative parish as they look to the dominant town for agricultural specialists, hospital service, and other professional leadership.

To delineate means to define. It can be recalled that one of the characteristics of the community is that it can be defined. It has geographic limitations. Among rural sociologists the delineation of the community has been done very effectively by determining common areas of trade and other areas of social interaction.

It was near the beginning of the century that a young sociologist accidentally discovered a method of delineating the rural trade community. Charles J. Galpin reported in 1911 on his work in Walworth County, Wisconsin:

> Take the village as the community center; start out from here on any road into the open country; you come to a home, and the deep wear of the wheels out of the yard toward the village indicates that this home naturally goes to this village for trade, doctor, post office, church, lodge, entertainment, high school; the next home the same, and the next and the next, until by and by you come to a home where the ruts run the other way and grass grows a little perhaps in the turn toward this village, and you find that this home goes to an adjoining town for its major associations; between these two homes is the bounding line of the community.[2]

Thus the trade area of a central town becomes the community area according to Galpin's discovery. This discovery has been explored by many researchers since that date, and the methods of community delineation have been based upon the assumption that where people derive their primary (that is, oft-repeated) services, such as food, school, church, doctor, entertainment, they will develop a community solidarity.

There are two primary ways of determining the trade or service area of a community. The first method is the modern sequel to Galpin's observations. Most states now place on county maps the average traffic flow per twenty-four hours at stated points along highways and secondary roads. The traffic-flow meter, which operates by photo-electric cell or with a rubber hose across the highway, is a common sight to the motorist. For a nominal sum, usually not more than a dollar, a traffic-flow map for a county can be obtained from the state highway department.[3] By finding on a given road the low point of traffic flow, it can be assumed that this is the point of division between two trade centers to which local residents go for their primary services.

Circumscribing a town on the map, one can find the low figure of traffic flow on each road. Connect these points by a line, and the trade area community is defined. Figure 17 illustrates the process, showing a section of the traffic-flow map of Ellis County, Texas. The communities and neighborhoods in Figure 1 (p. 46) were delineated by the traffic-flow process.

The second method of community delineation is to reverse the process of the traffic-flow method, that is, by starting in the trade-center village and working out to the extremity of the community, using the services needed by people for normal existence: economic, educational, religious, social, communicational, and professional. By talking with the persons in the trade center town, one can secure information on how far people come for the services. Take a map of the county to the grocer and ask him to spot on the map the homes in each direction whose

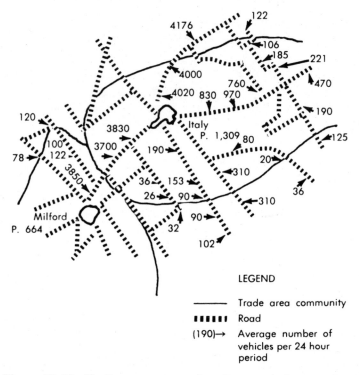

Figure 17. Traffic flow per twenty-four hour period. By finding on each highway and secondary road the point of the lowest traffic flow per twenty-four hour period, it can be assumed that that point is the dividing line between trade area communities. Connecting the points of lowest traffic flow around each town will determine the trade-area community.

residents trade at his store. Do the same for the garage operator, the service station operator, the banker, the doctor, the local newspaper editor. Ask the high school superintendent to plot on the map the homes at the extremity of the service area of the school. Connect the homes for the different services, drawing a line around the village or town. The areas for each service will not be

146

the same, but this will make a fairly well-defined configuration revealing the trade-area community.

It will be discovered that the larger the town, the larger will be the community. In simple general science there is an experiment demonstrating the power of a magnet. With a magnet beneath a sheet of paper, iron filings are dropped on the paper. Immediately the magnetic force is seen in the configuration of the iron filings around the magnetic poles. This is an elementary illustration of the pull of a trade center in a community. Naturally the more services a trade center can offer and the farther it is between trade-center towns, the larger will be the community. It is a safe hypothesis that a closely integrated larger parish, yoked field, enlarged charge, or extended ministry may be established within a community delineated in the above fashion. It is possible that racial, ethnic, or class factors will enter in, which will make for a lack of harmony. These factors do not appear in delineating the community by the trade-center area.

The enlarged community consists of one dominant town and two or more subdominant towns with their surrounding rural neighborhoods. The enlarged community is delineated in a similar manner to the community. The county is used as a basis for beginning the study. Many counties across the nation are becoming community-like since the central town, usually the county seat, supplies all of the services needed by the individual. In such a town will be one small hospital several lawyers, a public park, a library, and dealers in farm machinery, automobiles, and large appliances. Professional help such as an agricultural extension agent, a soil conservationist, and a home demonstration agent are in the larger town. Many central towns have the office of the regional Farm Bureau, Grange, Farmers' Union, or National Farmer's Organization.

A good way to start delineating an enlarged community is to take a map to the county agricultural extension agent. He will be able to point out the affinities of persons within the county and their dependence upon the central town. He can point out natural barriers, such as unbridged rivers, mountains, lakes, or forests, which keep people from making the central town their trade center for buying large items like farm machinery and automobiles.

Should there be two dominant towns in a county, it is quite likely there will be two enlarged communities. Figure 1 (p. 46) mapping Ellis County, Texas, shows clearly two enlarged communities in the county with the central towns of Waxahachie and Ennis, respectively.

It is possible that the enlarged community might reach beyond the county line. A rural neighborhood across the county line can be dependent upon one of the subdominant towns for primary trade and associations. The political boundary is not as strong as trade ties.

With the development of the consolidated school, it has been discovered that community boundaries and the extent of influence of the enlarged community are being redrawn to conform to the consolidated school boundaries. Ties made by children and young people in their associations in school activities are very strong.

The final test of a community and enlarged community delineation is by actually asking a series of questions of residents near the edge of what the researcher thinks is the boundary of the community, based upon his preliminary study. Sometimes, to save travel time, the questionnaire is put into the hands of children and young people in school. This method is not as reliable as the actual house-to-house visit but will be sufficient to begin the work of a parish. Questions such as the following should be asked:

148

1. Where does the family buy groceries?
2. Where does the family go to movies?
3. Where does the family buy gasoline?
4. In case a piece of farm machinery is broken during harvest, where does one go to buy small repair parts?
5. Where does the family buy cars?
6. Where does the family go for a medical doctor?
7. Where does the family go if in need of hospitalization?
8. Where does the family go to church?
9. Where do the young people attend high school?
10. Where do the children go to elementary school?
11. Where does the family attend Farm Bureau, Grange, or Farmers' Union meetings?
12. Where does the mother in the home buy the winter wardrobe for herself and family?

Space can be left at the end of each sentence to write in the name of a town. It is possible to put the names of towns into the questionnaire and simply ask the persons to check one under each item.

Questions 1,2,3,4,6,8,10, and 11 are indicative of community relationships. These are primary, or oft-repeated, services and are usually available at the community trade center. Questions 5,7,9, and 12 are guides to the enlarged community. With the exception of attendance at high school, they are services which are not needed often. Consolidation of schools in many cases has made the dominant town in an enlarged community more important.

A little practice and careful observation in community delineation will aid the novice in rural sociology to become efficient in understanding the natural groupings of the area under study.

*Delineation of Neighborhood
and Community in the City*

The defining of the neighborhood and community in urban areas is more complicated than their counterparts in nonmetropolitan areas. In chapter 3 the urban neighborhood is dealt with in detail. The urban neighborhood may be defined as a distinctive geographic area within a city which is predominantly residential, of near the same socio-economic level, in which there is one elementary school, small businesses, one or more small shopping centers and several churches. Figure 5 (p. 60) gives the neighborhoods in a section of Dallas, Texas. The elementary school districts are the primary factors in determining the neighborhood. Most cities will establish elementary schools on the basis that no child will need to walk more than one-half mile to school. Therefore schools are located approximately one mile apart. Land use (zoning ordinances) may be a second determining factor for the neighborhood. The land-use map in Figure 24 (p. 166) helps to see something of the consistency of the school district and the type of land use in the area. There may be a rather consistent type of zoning in the area of the school district. This is accidental rather than planned.

An urban neighborhood church will draw, in many instances, from 40 to 60 percent of its members from a radius of one mile from the church. It has been discovered that urban parents tend to make friends with one another on the basis of the schools which their children attend. School contacts are rather intense in activities, parent-teacher associations, and dad's clubs. This principle holds through both elementary and high school. In high school, however, the interest shifts from the school parents in general, to the parents of children involved in various

150

school activities such as band, orchestra, dramatic clubs, sports, and so forth.

The possibility of interchurch cooperation can be explored on the neighborhood basis. In Figure 5 (p. 60) it will be observed that there are numerous churches of different denominations within each neighborhood. In few instances are there two churches of the same denomination.

The urban community is defined in chapter 3 as, "The urban community is composed of two or more urban neighborhoods in which the socio-economic level of its residents is quite similar. There will be numerous churches of different denominations, several elementary schools, usually one junior high and one senior high school though the schools may draw from several urban communities." Figure 5 also outlines the urban communities of a section of Dallas. There are three communities in the area covered by the map. There is one high school and junior high school in the area, though two high schools and junior high schools serve the area.

The socio-economic levels, and residential levels of the Burgess concentric zone theory are evident in the region. The lower one-third of the area is the oldest part, the center one-third is marked by transition, and the upper third is still in the process of population increase due primarily to apartment building. Further analysis of the area in this chapter will assist in a better understanding of the community delineating process.

Within each of the communities of the region under study there could be a group ministry or larger parish. The organizations could be denominational or interdenominational.

The City Planning Department is an invaluable source of information. All cities have extensive departments of planning with a staff of specialists who have compiled massive data, and keep the information up to date. Most departments will have one member of the planning staff assigned to a particular section of the city. An hour's conversation with such a specialist discussing a section of the city can be quite productive.

City chambers of commerce usually maintain a department of planning. They keep accurate records of growth, population movements, economic trends, and projections for population expansion.

Population Analysis

The mission of the church is to serve people. What happens to population is of vital importance to the church. Population growth, decline, or internal change in racial, ethnic, or socio-economic structure alter the needs for ministry. In this section only the basic processes for population analysis are discussed. With some practice and study ministers and laymen may obtain information in relation to population which will assist in cooperative parish development. It is necessary to divide the analysis into two sections: (1) population analysis in town and country areas, and (2) population analysis in cities.

1. *Population analysis in town and country areas.* The unit for study in town and country areas is the county (or parish in Louisiana). Three separate U.S. census reports are available for each state. They may be purchased at nominal price or found in most public or school libraries. The reports are PC (1) A. *Number of Inhabitants,* PC (1) B. *General Population Characteristics,* PC (1) C. *General Social and Economic Characteristics.* Information is given in many categories, but basic to studies in conjunction with parish development are the county—county subdivisions which will be reported for twenty-eight states as *minor civil*

divisions, and for twenty-one states *census county divisions.* Alaska is reported by *boroughs,* and the individual town or city. Figure 18 is an illustration of Nevada County, Arkansas, showing minor civil divisions. They have been numbered for our purpose, and the numbers correspond with the numbers in Table 1, which gives the population changes for minor civil divisions over a fifty-year period. Basic information is available for the county for total population, rural farm, rural nonfarm, Negro, and persons with Spanish origin.

Nevada County, Arkansas, in 1920 had 21,934 inhabitants. In 1970 there were 10,111 inhabitants, or a 54 percent loss in fifty years. Though this loss is larger than many counties in America, it is quite typical of approximately one-half of the counties in the nation. There were in 1970, 3,278 Negroes in the county, or approximately one-third of the total population. The population is divided, approximately one-third urban (using as the definition of urban, all towns of more than 2,500 persons) and two-thirds rural. Within the rural population there were in 1970, 2,370 white nonfarm, 1,816 white farm, 1,678 Negro nonfarm, and 371 Negro farm.

Loss in population occurred in all the townships between 1960 and 1970 except Missouri and Georgia, which had a slight increase. The city of Prescott gained 388 in the decade. Georgia Township gained 45 in the ten-year period.

The age-sex distribution in Nevada County (see Figure 19) for white and Negro populations shows several interesting features. The small number of children under 5 years of age reveals a low birthrate in the white population. There was in 1970 a fertility ratio of 348. The fertility ratio is the number of children under 5 years of age for each one thousand women between the ages of 15 and 44.

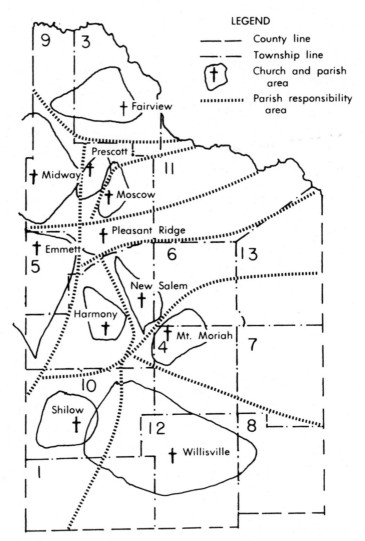

Figure 18. The above map of Nevada County, Arkansas, is illustrative of four major areas of research in preparation for a cooperative parish: (1) location of all churches in the denominations involved, (2) location of parish area of each church. (3) parish responsibility lines, and (4) township lines and township numbers. Table 1. shows the population trend by townships.

NEVADA COUNTY, ARKANSAS
Table 1. Population changes by county subdivisions, 1920-70

No.	Township Town or City	1920	1930	1940	1950	1960	1970	Change 1920-70	% Change 1920-70	Change 1960-70	% Change 1960-70
	TOTAL	21,934	20,407	19,869	14,781	10,700	10,111	−11,823	−53.9	−589	−5.5
1.	Alabama tp	1,116	1,125	948	687	403	394	−722	−64.6	−9	−2.2
2.	Albany tp	1,464	2,194	1,467	925	492	470	−994	−67.8	−22	−4.5
3.	Boughton tp	1,224	1,046	903	678	446	395	−829	−67.7	−51	−11.4
4.	Caney tp	1,277	1,145	1,390	931	620	560	−717	−56.1	−40	−9.7
5.	Emmet tp	1,182	1,007	1,020	782	633	599	−583	−49.3	−34	−5.4
	Emmet t	420	387	465	482	474	433	13	3.0	−41	−8.6
6.	Georgia tp	758	675	651	408	182	227	−531	−70.0	45	24.7
7.	Jackson tp	1,173	867	644	379	265	196	−977	−83.2	−69	−26.0
8.	Leake tp	742	897	834	554	325	202	−540	−72.7	−123	−37.8
9.	Missouri tp	5,635	5,814	6,188	5,741	4,823	4,873	−762	−13.5	50	1.0
	Prescott c	2,691	3,033	3,177	3,960	3,533	3,921	1,230	45.7	388	11.0
10.	Parker tp	1,908	1,615	1,484	888	514	501	−1,399	−73.6	−13	−2.5
11.	Redland tp	1,545	1,126	1,129	775	516	452	−1,093	−70.7	−91	−12.4
12.	Taylor tp	1,934	2,188	2,211	1,423	998	760	−1,174	−60.7	−238	−23.8
13.	Union tp	1,227	1,150	1,000	610	483	482	−745	−61.4	−1	−0.2

Negro population: 1960, 3,857; 1970, 3,278
Rural nonfarm white population: 1970, 2,370; Negro 1,678
Rural farm white population: 1970, 1,816; Negro 371

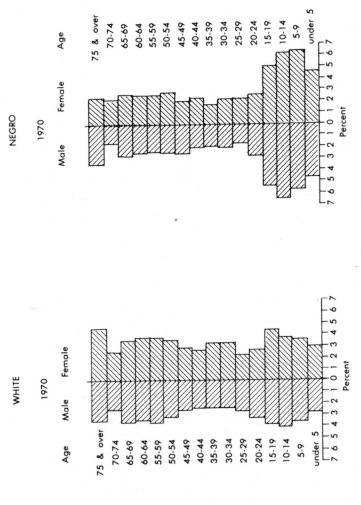

Figure 19. Age-sex distribution for White and Negro population in Nevada County, Arkansas, 1970.

In the Negro population there are many more children under 5 and a fertility ratio of 569. In both white and Negro populations there is a loss in population in the 20-24 age bracket. This is an indication that there are not sufficient job opportunities for persons in the county upon completion of high school. The age-sex graphs for a census tract in Dallas, Texas (Figure 23, p. 164) reveals dramatically the great increase in population in the 20-24 year bracket. Many of the young adults in the city are migrants from rural counties of America.

Nevada County, Arkansas, in both the white and Negro populations, has a disproportionately large number of persons 50 years of age or older.

The median school year completed for persons 25 years of age or older in Nevada County is 8.7 years. Twenty-seven percent of the population over 25 years has completed high school. Only 12 percent of the Negro population has completed high school.

The median income for all men 16 years of age or older for the county in 1970 was $3,990. For women in the labor force, $2,617.

The brief analysis of population in Nevada County, Arkansas is illustrative of the type of information which aids in planning a program of ministry in a given geographic area. It is quite obvious that one of the basic theses of this book is borne out in Nevada County, e. g., where there has been a serious change in population, racial or ethnic groups, and socio-economic levels, it is proper to consider a cooperative parish as a viable and effective means of ministry.

2. *Population analysis in cities.* The basic sources of information in cities of 50,000 population or more is the census tract. The census tract is a relatively small unit within the city, and data are given for each unit. Figure 20

Figure 20. Census tracts of East Dallas.

is a map of a segment of the city of Dallas, Texas, showing census tracts. Each tract is numbered to correspond with the numbers reported in the census information.

For the purpose of illustrating some aspects of urban population analysis a section of Dallas has been selected. The section has rather distinct boundaries being bordered on the west by Central Expressway, a four-to eight-lane, limited access thoroughfare; on the east by White Rock Lake; on the north by Northwest Highway, a three-to four-lane thoroughfare; and on the south by Thorton Freeway, an eight-lane, limited access thoroughfare, and an industrial district. In 1970 the entire area had 100,172 population. Part of the southern portion of the area has remained relatively stable in the census period 1960 to 1970, but the northern area has had a large increase due primarily to the construction of many apartment houses. There was a loss within the total area of 15,792 persons between 1960 and 1970. This was primarily due to industrial development in the extreme southern section of the area. Within the entire area there are fifty-seven churches of all denominations and four church-related institutions. The churches are located on Figure 21. Each church is numbered as an index for identification. The list is not published here, to save space. There are a total of seventeen Baptist churches of different branches, seven United Methodist, four Presbyterian, four Lutheran, three Disciples of Christ, three Church of Christ, two United Church of Christ, two Episcopal, and one each United Church of Practical Christianity, Roman Catholic, Greek Orthodox, Nazarene, Assembly of God, and nine churches of various sect groups.

Some of the population characteristics for one census tract are illustrated in Figure 22. This information needs to be tabulated for each census tract in assisting planners

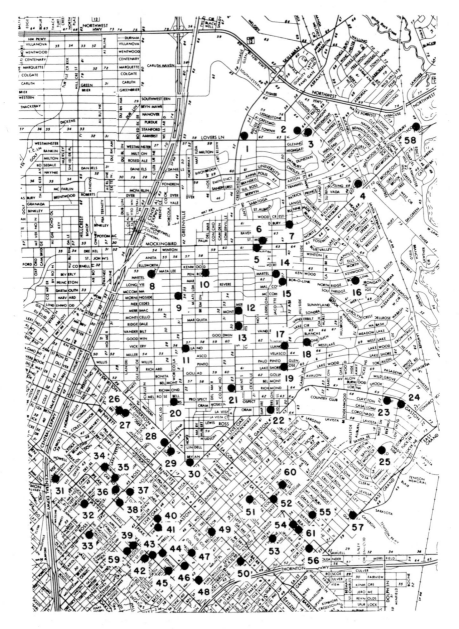

Figure 21. Churches of all denominations in East Dallas.

160

TRACT OOI3-B

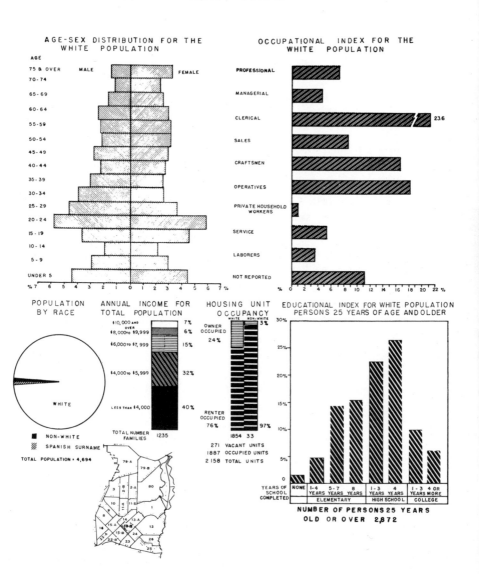

Figure 22. Population characteristics for census tract 13-B in East Dallas.

161

for cooperative parishes to understand more fully what the area under study is like. It helps to be able to direct the program of the church to the needs of the people.

The age-sex distribution shows a high percentage of persons 20 to 24 years of age, and a fairly large population in each adult age bracket. There are few youth 10 to 14 years of age and comparatively few children. The largest number of persons, almost one-fourth of the population, is employed in clerical work, with craftsmen and operatives combined accounting for more than a third of the population. Of the 4,694 persons in the census tract there is a very small number who are persons of Spanish descent or Negro.

Forty percent of the wage earners earn less than $4,000 per year, and 32 percent earn between $4,000 and $6,000. Only 7 percent of the wage earners receive an annual income of $10,000 or more.

Seventy-six percent of the white population rent their dwellings, and 24 percent own their own homes. Of the nonwhite population, which is quite small, only 3 percent own their own homes and 97 percent rent.

There are 2,872 persons in the census tract 25 years of age or older. Only 6 percent have four years or more of college work. Ten percent have been to college for one to three years. Twenty-seven percent have completed four years of high school and 23 percent have completed from one to three years of high school. Approximately one-third of the adult population has eight years of education or less.

The obvious facts from the brief study of census tract 13-B reveals the church, if effective in the area, must gear its program to persons of low income, low educational levels, predominantly white, and in the clerical, sales, craftsmen, and operatives fields of employment.

In the East Dallas Area being used as an example of urban research, the most radical changes which have taken place are in census tracts 79-A and 25. Tract 79-A is located in the northern border of the area. In 1960 the tract had 2,201 population and 7,779 in 1970. Figure 23 graphs the age-sex distribution for census tract 79-A for the two census periods. One-half the population is between the ages of 20 and 34. Sixteen percent is female between the ages of 20 and 24. Within the census tract there have been erected during the past ten years a number of apartment houses. One large apartment complex is of the country club type providing a golf course, three swimming pools, tennis courts, and other recreational facilities. An effective ministry in this type of area is difficult. It requires the cooperation of all churches in the area. There are no churches within census tract 79-A. There are, however three strong churches in census tract 79-B, Zion Lutheran Church (Missouri Synod), Ridgewood Park United Methodist, and St. Paul's United Church of Christ (formerly Evangelical and Reformed).

Tract 25 is located on the extreme southern end of the area under study. In 1960 there was a population of 5,478 white and 3,688 Negro. By 1970 the figures had changed to 460 white and 4,251 Negro.

Land Use

Another area of major importance in studying the city is how land has been designated to be used. Most major cities have rigid land-use policies established by zoning regulations. A trip to the planning department of the city can provide the information for the study. Maps are available for examination showing how the city is zoned. Future zoning plans are available with a fair degree of accuracy

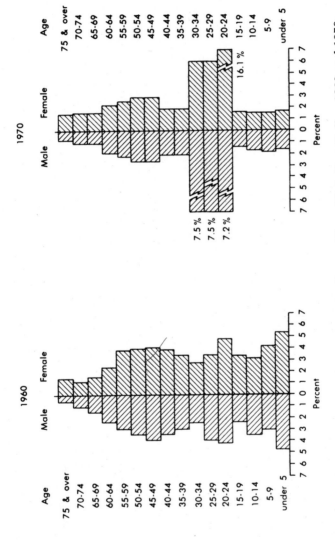

Figure 23. Age-sex distribution in Census Tract 79-A, East Dallas, 1960 and 1970.

as to what is anticipated in zoning. Figure 24 is a zoning map showing designated land use for the demonstration section of East Dallas.

Much of the lower one-fourth of the area has been zoned for multiple housing, light business, major business, and a small portion on the extreme south for heavy industry. In this region will be found a large medical complex with two hospitals, a dental school, and a school for nurses. There are two large doctors' buildings. There is much transition taking place in replacing old single-family dwellings with apartment houses. The apartments appeal to families and young couples. There are also some very old apartments and old mansion-type homes which have been converted into apartments. These are occupied by families of low income.

The middle and upper part of the area under study is zoned for single-family dwellings, with the exception of spot zoning for apartments and businesses. The Burgess concentric zone theory of urban development is quite obvious in the entire region. Moving from the south to the north one finds an upward mobility in socio-economic and educational levels and a lowering of age levels.

Parish Responsibility Areas

The Protestant church has never taken seriously the geographic parish as has the Roman Catholic Church. Among Catholics definite boundaries are drawn for a local congregation. When a family moves into a parish they are expected to move their membership to that parish church. Protestantism has left to the individual the choice of which congregation he will join and to which congregation he will transfer his membership.

Protestants should, however, have parish responsibility

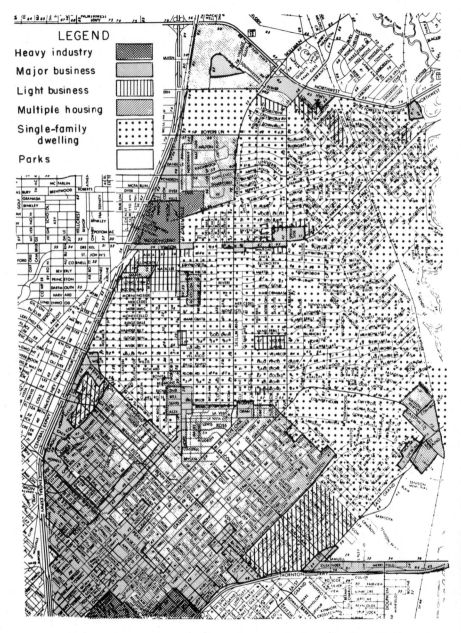

Figure 24. Land use and zoning regulations in East Dallas.

166

areas. That is, lines should be drawn between congregations, designating the area in which the local church is responsible for pastoral care and evangelism. Such parish boundaries do not confine the initiative of the individual but simply designate responsibility areas. In this manner no person is left outside the responsibility of a church. Many studies have revealed large sections of population outside the responsibility areas of existing congregations.

The first step in establishing responsibility areas is to discover the territories the churches are actually serving. This is done by asking the ministers to plot on a map the homes in which there are members of the local congregation. When the memberships are put together on a master map, a configuration of parish areas will take shape. Lines reaching the members on the extremity of the parish can be drawn around each church.

A more simple though not as accurate, method of determining parish areas is to prepare a sheet containing concentric circles. In the center is located the church. In each direction from the church the pastor will draw roads. He will place a dot on each road, locating the home of the farthest resident-member from the church. These dots are connected with an irregular line around the church. The area enclosed is the territory the church is actually serving. By placing on a master map the parish area, overlapping responsibility territory can be discovered, and areas unreached by any church will be revealed. Figure 18 (p. 154) shows the parish areas of the United Methodist churches of Nevada County, Arkansas.

The House-to-House Canvass

In obtaining accurate information on church potentials, nothing exceeds the house-to-house canvass in securing data from which the religious nature of a community can be discovered. To make a house-to-house canvass over an extensive territory, however, is a very large task involving a great deal of time. If the cooperative ministry has a full-time, employed staff member serving the whole area, the house-to-house canvass can be a project of that person. It is not wise to undertake a study on a wide scale with voluntary help until a cooperative parish is well under way. Sometimes in the enthusiasm of a newly organized parish, someone will suggest as the first joint project of the parish a census of the whole area. This sounds good, but when faced with the reality of making such a canvass, the people find that the spirit of the parish is frequently dampened. The matter of a parish-wide, house-to-house canvass should be postponed until the parish is well organized, and there is an adequate staff to give leadership to such an undertaking. Generally a parish is not ready for this type of work until it has been organized for at least two years.

When parish responsibility lines have been plotted on a map for each local church, there will usually be some part of the geographic region which is not being reached by any of the existing congregations. If this is the case, such as is found in townships 6, 11, and 13 of Nevada County, Arkansas (p. 154), a concentrated study can be made of such a section by all churches of the parish. A house-to-house survey should be made to determine how much church potential there is and why the residents of the area are not being reached by the existing congregations. Such a study may reveal the need for organizing another congregation. On the other hand, it may reveal a heavy ethnic or racial group who are members of another congregation and who are not cooperating in the parish.

Data on Church Organization

To obtain a broad understanding of the church in its existing state, data should be secured concerning the ministry, church building, parsonage or manse, historical information, organizational structure, church school, and other timely information. To secure such data, a questionnaire can be placed in the hands of each minister. He should be instructed to secure the assistance of a lay committee to answer all questions. When information from each church is compiled, the total church situation in a given area under study can be secured (see Appendix B).

Summary

By combining the knowledge gained in research for either a rural area or a section of a city it is possible to have a sound basis for considering cooperative parishes. Laymen and ministers need to have a broad knowledge of the physical features of land use, the natural neighborhoods and communities, the internal characteristics of population, and the future population potentials as they plan cooperatively to meet the religious needs of persons in their service area.

Little has been said in this chapter concerning the study of a local congregation. It is taken for granted that the use of a questionnaire (such as is found in Appendix B) will be applied for each of the congregations considering some type of cooperative parish. "Parish Development Aids" (Appendix C) also gives directions for coordinating the study of a local congregation with the study of an area.

Much time will be saved and a more logical basis secured for developing cooperative parishes and the proper program within the parish, if a thorough study of the area is made.

169

Postscript

As this book draws to a close the reader needs to be brought back to the basic premises on which it has been written. One may get lost in the mechanics of research methods, leadership procedures, sociology of rural and urban areas, and forms of the cooperative parish. These are mechanical devices to assist laymen and ministers to do a more effective work as churchmen. This book is based upon the following theses:

1. Professional ministry and organization are for the purpose of assisting the laity to be the church in worship, nurture, and at work in the world.

2. Persons tend to support ideas they have had the opportunity to help formulate. This respects the fundamental dignity of man as a creative being of God.

3. Persons will accept new ideas if they feel they are to their advantage. This concept, too, respects the dignity of man and his innate desire for improvement for himself and his church.

4. The cooperative parish in one of its varied forms may

offer a viable means of ministry where there has been a serious change in population, racial or ethnic groups, or socio-economic levels, and there are existing churches of one or more denominations.

5. Underlying all of the psychological and sociological concepts of parish development is the basic theological belief and conviction of the author that the main task of the church is to reach persons with the confrontation of the gospel and to assist persons to develop their lives around the central concept of Christianity as the servant community. The first title of the original document on parish development written by me was *Serve to Survive*. That thesis is still behind this book. Christianity is a faith which is based upon servanthood. The cooperative parish is corporate servanthood of the congregations in service to all persons and all needs of persons in the geographic area of the parish, and a part of the universal Christian church in the world. Survival is secondary—service is paramount!

Appendix A

CONSTITUTION OF
A LARGER PARISH

I. PURPOSE:

The purpose of this Larger Parish is to minister to all the people within its area through a program of activities that can best be planned and carried on with the cooperation of several churches.

II. STAFF:

1. The staff shall be composed of the parish director and ministers of churches and / or charges within the parish.
2. The director:
   a. Shall be responsible to the denominational executive and the parish council for developing and carrying on a total ministry to all the people within the parish.
   b. May also serve as pastor of one of the charges in the parish. If so, the time he gives to the work of his charge shall be equal to that given by a student minister to his charge.
3. Ministers appointed to charges within the parish shall

be responsible for developing and carrying on a total ministry to all the people within their charges, in co-operation with other charges of the parish and under the guidance and supervision of the parish director.

III. MEMBERSHIP:

The Larger Parish shall be composed of the following charges: Barlow, Beauregard, Gallman, and Georgetown. Any church within the area may participate in the work of the Larger Parish upon approval by the parish council. It shall be entitled to the same membership on the council as any church in the parish, and shall share in the responsibilities of the parish program.

IV. PARISH COUNCIL:

1. The Larger Parish Council shall be a program-planning body. It shall initiate, coordinate, and implement the program of the parish, and request financial support from participating churches.
2. The director of the Larger Parish shall be the executive officer of the parish council. He shall be responsible to the parish council.
3. The council shall be composed of two elected representatives from each church participating in the work of the parish, to be elected at the same time and in the same manner as at-large members of the administrative board of the local church.
4. The council may elect other persons from participating churches to membership on the council because of skills and knowledge or special interest in the work of the parish. They shall be elected for a term of one year, beginning in January.
5. Officers of the council shall be president, vice-president, secretary, and treasurer. They are to be lay people and elected in the January meeting for a term of one year. The executive committee of the parish council shall be composed of its officers. If a charge is not rep-

resented on the executive committee, one representative shall be added from that charge by the parish council.

6. The council shall meet bi-monthly, and in special session as called by the president or parish director.

7. All members of the staff shall be ex-officio members of the council and their attendance is requested at each meeting.

8. The council may establish such committees, commissions, and task forces as may be necessary for the implementation of its work. Members of these groups may come from any participating church of the parish.

V. FINANCES:

1. Each church and / or charge shall continue its local and denominational obligations as before it became a member of the Larger Parish.

2. Financial needs of the parish shall be budgeted by the parish council. These needs shall be in relationship to programs of the parish.

3. Each church shall be responsible to the Larger Parish only for amounts that have been pledged by the church or charge. However, each church is expected to share its part of the financial affairs of the parish.

4. All money for the Larger Parish shall be paid to the parish treasurer, who shall pay bills as authorized by the council.

5. The council shall give an itemized annual accounting of all receipts and disbursement to churches of the parish.

VI. AMENDMENTS:

1. Amendments of this constitution shall be made in one of the following ways:
   a. If notice is given to all members of the council prior to the meeting, the council may amend the constitution with a majority vote while in session.

b. If prior notice has not been given of an amendment offered in a meeting, but it receives unanimous approval of those present, it shall become effective immediately. If it does not receive unanimous approval, it must be held over to the next meeting for a majority vote only.

Appendix B

STUDY GUIDE

_____ District

_____ Pastor

_____ Address

A. *The Church in the Community.*
1. Name of church _____ Charge _____.
2. P.O. Address _____ Town _____
County _____ Township _____.
3. Number of churches on charge ____. (*A study guide should be prepared for each church on the charge.*)
4. The church is located in: open country_____; village or town _____; city _____. Population, if known _____ _____. If a city church, it is: downtown _____; residential _____; suburban _____; other (specify) ___

_____

_____.

5. If church is in town of 2,500 or less, or open country, from what distance can the church be reached with good roads?_____.

177

6. How far is the nearest church of the same denomination? _____ Blocks; _____ Miles.
7. Is the church well marked with a sign or signs? _____. A bulletin board? _____.
8. Does the charge provide a parsonage? Yes _____; No _____. How far from this church? _____ Blocks; _____ Miles.
9. Where is the pastor's study located? Church _____; Parsonage _____; None _____.
10. The minister:
    How many years have you served in the ministry?____.
    How many years in present charge? _____.
    How many charges have you served? _____.
    Education: Please fill in the following table:

	YEAR ATTENDED	NAME OF SCHOOL	YEAR GRADUATED	DIPLOMA OR DEGREE
High School				
College				
Seminary				
Other				

B. History and Organization.
1. In what year was the church organized? _____.
2. Has the church ever sponsored the formation of another church? Yes _____; No _____. A church school? Yes _____; No _____; Dates _____.
3. What is the status of the sponsored group at present? Active _____; Inactive _____; Dissolved _____.
4. This committee believes that a survey to determine the need of a new church should be conducted in the area of _____.

178

The boundaries of this area are:
a. Northern limits. Street or highway _____.
b. Eastern limits. Street or highway _____.
c. Southern limits. Street or highway _____.
d. Western limits. Street or highway _____.

C. *Building and Equipment.*

1. In what year was the present building erected? _____.
   Date when last finished (redecorated) inside? _____.
   Additions were added to building in the years _____.
2. What is the general condition of the church building (s) ?
   Good _____; Fair _____; Major repairs needed _____; Condemned _____.
3. What is the general condition of the parsonage? Good _____; Fair _____; Major repairs needed _____.
   List the major repairs needed _____
   _____.
4. How many rooms in the parsonage? _____. Do they provide adequate living space for the minister's family?
   Yes _____; No _____.
5. Does the parsonage have the following equipment: central heat _____; gas heat _____; refrigeration _____; electricity _____; plumbing complete _____; plumbing partial _____; power washer _____; complete furnishings _____; air conditioning _____.
6. Are the church buildings and equipment considered adequate for the needs of the congregation? Yes _____; No _____. Explain _____
   _____.

D. *Finances.*

1. How much was raised for all purposes last year? _____
   _____ (amount reported in last conference journal or denominational yearbook).
2. List the approximate amount of the budget raised last year from the following sources: (consult your church treasurer for accuracy).

179

Contributions of members through systematic giving $_____. Special offerings (such as Easter, Christmas, etc.) $_____. Endowments $_____
_____.

3. Is the church engaged in a special building fund campaign? Yes _____; No _____. If yes, give goal for campaign $_____; collected to date $_____
_____; pledged to date above collected $_____
_____.

4. How many members follow consistent giving? _____
(pay regularly to church weekly or monthly)

5. Is there an annual every-member canvass to secure pledges to underwrite the budget? Yes _____; No _____.

6. Has the church any indebtedness? Yes _____; No _____;
Amount $_____.

7. For what reason was the debt assumed? _____.
_____

8. How long has it been carried? _____. How is it being taken care of? _____.

9. If financial aid is received from outside the church, list where: Conference or association board of missions _____
_____; Sustentation or minimum salary fund _____
_____; General board of missions _____. Amount in current year $ _____. How many years has there been such aid? _____.

E. *Membership.*

1. Number of church members reported in last conference journal or year book _____.

2. Number of church members who do not live in the immediate vicinity of the church. These might be called nonresident members _____.

3. Number of people listed on the constituency roll or prospect roll _____.

4. What is the average attendance at Sunday morning church worship service for the past six months? _____. Evening service _____.

5. During the past five years, how many young people from this church have entered the ministry or mission field? _____.

F. Program and Organization.

1. Organizations: fill in the following listings:

	NUMBER OF GROUPS	MEMBERSHIP	NUMBER OF MEETINGS PER YEAR
Women's Organization			
Men's Organization			
Youth Organization			

2. Check if committees are organized and functioning in the following areas:

	Organized	Functioning
Evangelism	Yes__; No__	Yes__; No__
Education	Yes__; No__	Yes__; No__
Missions	Yes__; No__	Yes__; No__
Christian Social Concerns	Yes__; No__	Yes__; No__
Finance	Yes__; No__	Yes__; No__
Worship	Yes__; No__	Yes__; No__

3. Does the church practice the rotation system in the official board or other governing body? Yes__; No__.
4. Activities: fill in the following inventory:

	Yes	No
Public worship every Sunday morning		
Public worship every Sunday night		

THE PARISH DEVELOPMENT PROCESS

	Yes	No
Services two Sunday mornings per month		
Services one Sunday per month		
Regular midweek service		
Special evangelistic services held last year		
Special Holy Week observance		
Daily vacation church school in last year		
Weekday religious education for children		
Mission study classes held		
Church membership preparation classes		
Envelopes used weekly or monthly for offering		
Regularly adopted church budget		
Permanent membership record		
Alphabetical membership record		
Evangelistic visitation teams		
Lord's Acre program		
Regular choir (4 or more voices)		
Children's choir		
Delegates to youth camp		
Clinic or dispensary		

	Yes	No
Supervised playground or gym		
Monthly family nights		
Weekly church bulletin (enclose a copy)		
Weekly or monthly church paper (enclose a copy)		
Regular radio program		
Regular television program		
Regular newspaper space bought		
Sponsor Boy Scouts		
Sponsor Girl Scouts		
Part of group ministry		
Church is member of interdenominational council, either city or county		

List here the preaching schedule if above does not apply

CHECK HYMNBOOK USED:

	SUNDAY SCHOOL	CHURCH
Official denominational hymnal		
Other (write in name)		

(TO BE PREPARED BY CHURCHES LOCATED IN COM-
MUNITIES OF *2,500* POPULATION AND LESS, INCLUD-
ING OPEN COUNTRY)

G. *The Church and Its Surroundings.*

2. How many (more or less) businesses are there in your
   town now than ten years ago? More _____; Less _____.
   (Inquire of longtime residents)
2. What has been the (increase or decrease) in public school
   enrollment in the past ten years? Increase _____; Decrease _____.
3. Check the following considering the *majority* of people
   in the community:

	Town	Distance
Where do they buy groceries?		
Where do they buy cars?		
Where do they bank?		
Where do children attend high school?		
Where do children attend elementary school?		
Where can a doctor be secured?		
Where do they go for hospital service?		

4. Check the following if a community problem:

__Commercial recreation   __Lack opportunities for youth
__Poverty or unemployment   __Lack community pride
__Poor roads   __Underchurched
__Overchurched   __Juvenile delinquency
__Poor public schools   __Inadequate leadership
__Community conflict

5. Number of church members with residence in community who commute daily outside community for employment _____.

6. Is there a general migration of young people out of the community? Yes _____; No _____. Explain _____
_____.

7. Is there any type of community coordinating organization made up of various religious and secular organizations? Yes _____; No _____. If yes, does this church belong to it? Yes _____; No _____.

(TO BE PREPARED BY ALL CHURCHES)

MAP (*locating church, churches of other denominations, abandoned churches, towns*)

On this page sketch a map of the territory around the church
of this questionnaire for a distance of five miles in each direction. Locate the following items on the map:

1. Major highways or streets (name and number them).
2. Other churches of same denomination in the area (name
   them on map).
3. Churches of other denominations (names).
4. Abandoned churches of same denomination (name them).
5. If a country church, name and locate towns in area.

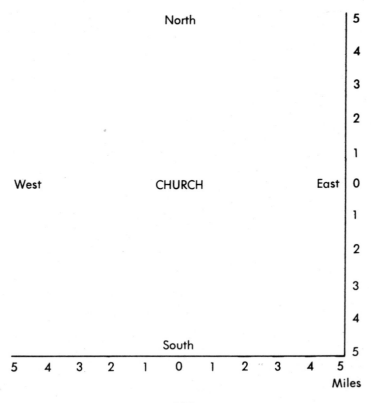

APPENDIX B

INSTRUCTIONS:

Each circle represents one-half mile radius from the church.

1. Locate the church at the center of the circle at intersection of North-South and East-West lines.

2. Draw lines representing streets or roads leading from church.

3. Place a dot at the location of each church family living on each road.

4. Connect the dots at farthest extremity, drawing a line around the circles. This is an outline of the parish boundary.

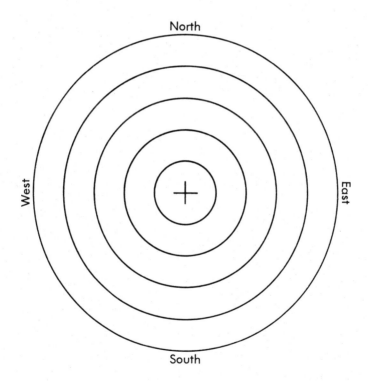

187

Appendix C

PARISH DEVELOPMENT AIDS

This section is a six-session course of study designed to assist laymen and pastors to work through a self-study to lead to the developing, organizing, and putting into operation a cooperative parish. The philosophy behind the study is described in chapter 5, "Establishing the Cooperative Parish." See especially Figure 15, page 95.·

The textbook for the course is this volume, *The Parish Development Process*. Additional readings are listed in the bibliography in this book.

PRELIMINARY PREPARATION

The leaders of the class will need to make the following preparation prior to the first session.

1. Secure a good map of the potential cooperative parish area. In town and country areas such a map may be obtained from the state highway department for a nominal fee. A map to the one-half or full scale is sufficient. In the city, maps for the segment to be studied may be obtained at the city planning department or from private firms who will reproduce the

section of the city asked for in any size desired (look in the Yellow Pages of the phone directory under "Maps").

2. For a study in town and country areas secure from the state highway department a traffic-flow map for the county or counties to be studied.

3. For a study in the city secure from the city planning department a map showing land-use indicating zoning regulations. Also secure a map showing projected street construction.

4. For the city area study obtain from the city public school office a map showing elementary, junior high, and high school districts. Ask for the school enrollments for the past five years for the schools in the area to be studied. If available obtain enrollments for ethnic and racial groups.

5. For the city study secure from the U.S. Census Bureau the books *Census Tracts* and *Block Statistics*. Census books may be obtained at nominal price from Superintendent of Documents, U.S. Government Printing Office, Washington, D. C., 20402. They are available for sale at any Department of Commerce field office, located in most major cities. Most public libraries will have the documents.

6. For town and country areas secure the census books *Number of Inhabitants* (PC(1), *General Population Characteristics* PC(2), and *General Social and Economic Characteristics* PC(3). These reports will be for the entire state and information is reported by counties.

7. In town and country areas secure from the county superintendent of schools and from local school district offices the enrollment for schools over a five-year period and a map showing elementary, junior high, and high school districts.

8. A questionnaire similar to the one found in Appendix B needs to be circulated to each church in the potential cooperative parish area. A committee in each church will need to fill in all information in the questionnaire.

9. The directives in chapter 8 of this book in regard to research need to be reviewed and carefully followed.

10. All persons to be in the study will need to have read the text before the first session.

SESSION I: DISCOVERING NEEDS

Objective: To discover through analysis and discussion the needs of the church within the region under study.

Reports need to be made of studies that have been done, the material on the questionnaires reported, and the basic geographical features of the area under study. Some areas of discussion may be:

1. What is the general trend of churches in the area in regard to membership, church school enrollment, church school attendance?

2. How many cooperating churches are there in the area? Where are they located? What other churches of different denominations are there? What are their strengths? What churches of different racial or ethnic groups are there? What are their strengths?

3. Where are the members of the churches in the area living? What is the parish area of each church? (The parish areas need to be plotted on a map as described in chapter 8, Figure 18.)

4. What are the charge arrangements in the area? Where do the ministers live? (Plot this information on the map.)

5. What can be discovered about the individual churches: (a) membership, (b) church school enrollment, (c) church school average attendance, (d) budgets, (e) organizations—women's and men's groups, youth groups, denominational boards, (f) worship schedules, (g) building? What are the trends over the past twenty years in the above items?

6. Who are the ministers of the area? What are their pastoral responsibilities?

SESSION II: DISCOVERING NATURAL SOCIOLOGICAL AREAS

Objective: To assist persons to understand in general the nature of the area under study either town and country or urban, with varying sociological forces which have a direct bearing upon the work of the church. Chapters 2 and 3 of the text need to be thoroughly mastered.

In preparation for Session Two a large map of the region

should be prepared which will have on it some of the information discovered in Session One and other relevant data.

Locality groups I, II, III, and IV need to be defined for town and country areas, and locality groups V and VI need to be defined for urban areas.

Question guides are divided for persons studying town and country areas and for persons studying urban areas.

Some topics for discussion by persons in town and country areas:

1. What are the locality groups II (rural communities) as defined by study of the area through questionnaires and traffic-flow maps? (See chs. 2 and 8)

2. Where are the rural neighborhood congregations (locality group 1)?

3. To what communities do the rural neighborhood churches belong?

4. Are the pastoral charges arranged so as to take advantage of most logical sociological forces in the area?

5. Population analysis:
    a) Define the population census areas or townships.
    b) Trace by minor civil divisions (census areas, townships, towns, and cities) the trend in population over a period of fifty years.
    c) What ethnic and / or racial groups are there?
    d) What is the age-sex distribution? Fertility ratio?
    e) What is the rural farm, rural nonfarm, and urban population?

6. Economic analysis:
    a) How does the majority of the people make a living?
    b) What are the land ownership patterns? What is the farm rental pattern?
    c) What are the major industries of the region?
    d) Are there changing economic patterns in the area?
    e) Are there job opportunities for young people who want to begin their careers?

7. What effect do the forces mentioned above have on the churches in the region?

192

Some topics for discussion by persons in urban areas:

a) What are the locality groups V (urban neighborhood) and VI, urban communities?

b) Where are the elementary, junior high, and high schools located?

c) What have been the school enrollments over the past five years?

d) What has been the change in racial or ethnic school enrollments in the past five years?

e) Population analysis:

(1) Define the census tracts of the area.

(2) What have been the changes in census tract population over the past twenty years?

(3) What ethnic or racial groups are there?

(4) What has been the change in racial and ethnic groups in twenty years?

(5) What is the age-sex distribution comparing two census periods? What changes have taken place in the ten year-period? What is the fertility ratio? How do the changes affect the work of the church?

(6) What is the occupational classification of the people in the census tracts? How does the census tract occupational profile compare with the occupational profile of the church membership of the churches of the area?

f) What are the zoning ordinances in the area? How is land use designated? What plans are there for change?

g) What are the plans for future development of streets and traffic patterns?

h) What is the condition of housing in the area? What are the estimated values of housing? What percent of the homes are renter-and owner-occupied?

i) Attempt to interpret the information in the light of what the various phases of the analysis mean for the churches under study.

SESSION III: DEFINITIONS AND ALTERNATIVES
FOR COOPERATIVE PARISHES

Objective: To assist persons to understand the types of cooperative parishes, the philosophy undergirding them, and to explore what types of parish structures may be applicable for the area under study. Text: chapter 4.

1. Define the consolidated or merged church, the extended ministry, the larger charge, the larger parish, the group ministry, the federated church, the yoked field, and two congregations in one building.

2. What are the advantages of each type of cooperative parish listed in question one?

3. What was the motivating aspect for Harlow S. Mills in beginning the larger parish?

4. What was the vision of Don Benedict for the East Harlem Protestant Parish?

5. What did Aaron Rapking envision as the motivation for, and advantages of, the group ministry?

6. In studying the map of the region under consideration (either town and country or urban) what possibilities are seen for one of the types of cooperative parishes in question 1?

SESSION IV: ESTABLISHING COOPERATIVE PARISHES

Objective: To understand the process by which persons are incorporated into planning for the beginning of a cooperative parish. Text: chapter 5.

1. What is meant by a construct of social action?

2. In the light of the discussion in chapter 5, define the following and apply the definition to the geographic area being studied: (a) social system boundary, (b) convergence of interests, (c) prior social situation, (d) professionals living in the system, (e) professionals outside the system, (f) the problem situation, (g) relevant social systems, (h) the initiating set, (i) legitimation, (j) diffusion set, (k) goals, (l) evaluation.

3. Who is responsible for stimulating interest in the cooperative parish?

4. Is further research needed for the cooperative parish? If so, what information needs to be obtained? Who can be of assistance in getting and interpreting the information?

5. Define clearly the basic goals and objectives of the cooperative parish.

6. How can a large number of persons be brought into planning for the cooperative parish?

7. Will there be a need for a constitution? If so, who is given responsibility for it, and what should it contain?

8. Is there a need to set up a series of meetings leading up to the final adoption of a plan to begin the cooperative parish? If so, define the nature of the meetings, programs, delegations, and set tentative dates.

9. What relationship do the denominational regional representatives have to the planning process, and how are they involved?

SESSION V: THE COOPERATIVE PARISH AT WORK

Objective: To gain a clear understanding of how a cooperative parish functions. Text: chapter 6.

1. Relate the goals and objectives discussed in the previous session to the program of the cooperative parish. A program is designed to implement the goals and objectives.

2. How is a council in a cooperative parish selected? Define the council's responsibilities.

3. List some possible areas in which a cooperative parish can work with simultaneous action in the various congregations. What advantages can there be in such action?

4. Describe a parish paper. What should its subject matter be? Who should edit such a paper? How should it be financed? How and to whom should it be circulated?

5. What is a "parish day"? Consider some of its values.

6. What type of budget should there be for a cooperative parish? How is it determined? How do the congregations share in the raising of the budget?

7. What types of committees are needed in the cooperative parish?

8. With what areas of community service should the co-operative parish be concerned, and how should the parish as such work in such enterprises?

9. Examine the life-support systems listed in chapter 6, and examine the community under study to measure how well each system is being supplied. How would a cooperative parish assist in providing for more effective life-support systems?

SESSION VI: LEADERSHIP

Objective: to consider the various leadership roles in a cooperative parish and their relationships. Text: chapter 7.

Some areas for consideration:

1. State the various leadership roles in a cooperative parish such as parish director and official board of each local church.

2. Define the responsibilities of each person or group which has leadership responsibilities.

3. What are some of the fundamental principles of good personnel management?

4. What is a job description? How does it apply to a parish staff?

5. List some of the problems which are likely to appear among leaders in a cooperative parish and how they can be solved.

6. What is the place and function of denominational regional executives, such as a district superintendent, to the leadership of a cooperative parish?

7. What is the relationship between the parish council and the official board of each local church?

8. List some of the qualifications which a parish director needs to have to equip him for his position.

9. Discuss the types of staff meetings which need to be held by a cooperative parish. What is the philosophy behind each type of meeting?

10. What needs to be done on a denominational level to insure the continuance of a cooperative parish over a long period of time?

Notes

CHAPTER I

1. Harlow S. Mills, *The Making of A Country Parish* (New York: Missionary Education Movement of United States and Canada, 1914), pp. 26, 28.

2. *Ibid.*, pp. 29, 30, 33.

3. *Ibid.*, pp. 13, 15, 18, 20.

4. Bruce Kenrick, *Come Out The Wilderness* (New York: Harper & Brothers, 1962), p. 4.

5. *Ibid.*, pp. 10, 11. For a full description of the East Harlem Protestant Parish see, George W. Webber, *God's Colony in Man's World* (Nashville: Abingdon Press, 1960).

6. Marvin T. Judy and Murlene O. Judy, *The Multiple Staff Ministry* (Nashville: Abingdon Press, 1969), ch. 1, "A Doctrine of the Multiple Staff Ministry."

7. For an excellent treatment of a theology of the parish see Earl D. C. Brewer, Theodore H. Runyan, Jr., Barbara B. Pittard, Harold McSwain, *Protestant Parish* (Atlanta: Communicative Arts Press, 1962), ch. 2.

CHAPTER II

1. Lowry Nelson, *Rural Social Systems* (New York: American Book Company, 1955), p. 187.

2. John H. Kolb, *Emerging Rural Communities: Group Relations in Rural Society, A Review of Wisconsin Research in Action* (Madison: The University of Wisconsin Press, 1959), p. 42.

197

3. R.M. MacIver, *Community: A Sociological Study* (New York: The Macmillan Co., 1928), p. 22.

4. Kenyon L. Butterfield, *Mobilizing the Rural Community*. Extension Bulletin No. 23 (Massachusetts Agricultural College, 1918), p. 9.

5. Dwight Sanderson, *Locating the Rural Community*. Cornell reading course for the farm (New York State College of Agriculture, 1920), lesson 158, p. 417.

6. Dwight Sanderson, *The Rural Community: The Natural History of a Sociological Group* (Boston: Ginn and Co., 1932), p. 481.

7. John H. Kolb and Edmund deS. Brunner, *A Study of Rural Society*, 4th ed. (Boston: Houghton Mifflin, 1952), p. 233.

8. Karl A. Fox and T. Krishna Kumar, "The Functional Economic Area: Delineation and Implications for Economic Analysis and Policy," mimeographed (Ames: Iowa State University, Department of Economics, March 20, 1965), p. 13.

9. Charles J. Galpin, "The Social Anatomy of an Agricultural Community" (Madison: Agricultural Experiment Station of the University of Wisconsin, Research Bulletin No. 34, May 1915).

CHAPTER III

1. For a fuller discussion of these concepts see Noel P. Gist and Sylva Fleis Fava, *Urban Society*, 5th ed. (New York: Thomas Y. Crowell Company, 1964), pp. 10 ff.

2. See Robert E. Park, Ernest W. Burgess, and R. D. McKenzie, *The City* (Chicago: University of Chicago Press, 1925), p. 51.

3. Homer Hoyt, *The Structure and Growth of Residential Neighborhoods in American Cities* (Washington, D.C.: Federal Housing Administration, 1939), ch. 6.

4. C. D. Harris and Edward L. Ullman, "The Nature of Cities," *The Annals*, 245 (November, 1945), 7-17.

5. Charles P. Loomis and Zona K. Loomis, *Modern Social Theories* (Princeton, N.J.: D. Van Nostrand Co., 1961), p. 3.

6. For a detailed discussion of *"community"* see the bibliography at the end of the book, and especially Roland L. Warren, *The Community in America* (Chicago: Rand McNally & Co., 1963). Warren uses the social systems concept as a frame of reference for community structure.

CHAPTER IV

1. Edmund deS. Brunner, *The Larger Parish, a Movement or an Enthusiasm?* (New York: The Institute of Social and Religious Research, 1934), p. 67.

2. Mark Rich, *The Larger Parish, an Effective Organization for Rural Churches* (Ithaca, N.Y.: Cornell University Extension Bulletin No. 408, 1939), p. 4.

3. Aaron H. Rapking, "Pioneering in the Kingdom of God," (unpublished), ch. 7. Used by permission.

4. Douglas W. Johnson, *A Study of Methodist Group Ministries and Larger Parishes in the Inner City* (Chicago: Chicago Home Missionary and Church Extension Society, Rock River Conference of The Methodist Church, 1966).

CHAPTER V

1. Adapted from George M. Beal, Ross C. Blount, Ronald C. Powers, and W. John Johnson, *Social Action and Interaction in Program Planning* (Ames: Iowa State University Press, 1966), p. 6.

CHAPTER VII

1. For a detailed discussion on human relations between the employed professionals within the church see Marvin T. Judy in cooperation with Murlene O. Judy, *The Multiple Staff Ministry* (Nashville: Abingdon Press, 1969). In addition to treating a wide range of staff relationships chapter 11 is specifically directed toward "The Multiple Staff in the Cooperative Parish."

2. *Ibid.*, p. 248, a sample of a statement of personnel policies.

3. *Ibid.*, pp. 255-72, sample job descriptions for employed church professionals.

4. *Ibid.*, pp. 251-55, a sample brochure on "Interpreting the Work of the Staff to the Congregation."

5. *Ibid.*, pp. 220-35, a more involved discussion of the staff meetings.

6. Murray H. Leiffer, *Changing Expectations and Ethics in the Professional Ministry* (Evanston, Ill.: Bureau of Social and Religious Research, Garrett Theological Seminary, 1969).

7. George R. Terry, *Principles of Management* (Homewood, Ill.: Richard D. Irwin, 1956), p. 342.

8. *Ibid.*, p. 345.

CHAPTER VIII

1. Brunner, *The Larger Parish.* p. 67.

2. Charles J. Galpin, *First Wisconsin Country Life Conference* (Madison: University of Wisconsin, 1911), p. 12.

3. An excellent base map for a county can be secured from the state highway department. When ordering, state the county and size. Most highway departments have "full-size" (one inch to the mile), "half-size" (one-half inch), and "one-quarter size" (one-quarter inch). Such maps list all roads, schools, churches, cemeteries, rivers, business houses, residences, and towns and cities.

Bibliography

Altshuler, Alan A. *The City Planning Process: A Political Analysis.* Reprint of 1965 ed. Ithaca, N.Y.: Cornell University Press, 1969.

Beal, George M.; Blount, Ross C.; Powers, Ronald C.; and Johnson, W. John. *Social Action and Interaction in Program Planning.* Ames: Iowa State University Press, 1966.

Biddle, Williams W., and Biddle, Loureide J. *The Community Development Process—The Rediscovery of Local Initiative.* New York: Holt, Rinehart and Winston, 1965.

Biddle, William W. *The Cultivation of Community Leaders.* New York: Harper & Brothers, 1953.

Bill, Harry. *Why Organizations Fail: The Story of a Rent Strike.* Berkley: University of California Press, 1971.

Brewer, Earl D. C.; Runyan, Theodore H.; Pittard, Barbara; McSwain, Harold, *Protestant Parish.* Atlanta: Communicative Arts Press, 1962.

Brownell, Baker. *The Human Community: Its Philosophy and Practice for a Time of Crisis.* New York: Harper & Brothers, 1950 (o.p.).

Brunner, Edmund deS. *The Larger Parish, a Movement or an Enthusiasm?* New York: The Institution of Social and Religious Research, 1934 (o. p.).

Chapin, F. Stuart, Jr., and Weiss, Shirley F., eds. *Urban Growth Dynamics.* New York: John Wiley & Sons, 1962.

Chermayeff, Serge, and Alexander, Christopher. *Community and Privacy: Toward a New Architecture of Humanism.* Garden City, N.Y.: Doubleday, Anchor Books, 1965.

201

Clark, M. Edward: Malcomson, William L.; and Molton, Warren Lane. *The Church Creative.* Nashville: Abingdon Press, 1967.

Clark, Terry N., ed. *Community Structure and Decision-making: Comparative Analysis.* San Francisco: Chandler Publishing Co., 1968.

Community Survey, The. Soc. 15. Ames: Iowa State University of Science and Technology, 1964.

Garrison, Edwin R. *The Parish For the New Age.* 601 Riverview Avenue Dayton, Ohio, 45406, 1972.

Gibbs, Jack P. *Urban Research Methods.* New York: Van Nostrand Reinhold Co., 1961.

Gist, Noel P., and Fava, Sylvia Fleis. *Urban Society.* 5th ed. New York: Thomas Y. Crowell Company, 1964.

Glasse, James D. *Putting It Together in the Parish.* Nashville: Abingdon Press, 1972.

Gore, William J., and Hodapp, Leroy C. *Change in the Small Community: An Interdisciplinary Survey.* New York: Friendship Press, 1967 (o. p.).

Hersey, Paul, and Blanchard, Kenneth H. *Management of Organizational Behavior.* Englewood Cliffs, N.J.: Prentice-Hall, 1969.

Judy, Marvin T. *The Multiple Staff Ministry.* Nashville: Abingdon Press, 1969.

Keller, Suzanne. *The Urban Neighborhood: A Sociological Perspective.* New York: Random House, 1968.

Kelley, Arleon, ed. *Ecumenical Design: Imperatives for Action in Nonmetropolitan America.* New York: National Consultation on Church and Community Life (475 Riverside Drive, 10027), 1967 (o. p.).

Kenrick, Bruce. *Come Out the Wilderness: The Story of East Harlem Protestant Parish.* New York: Harper & Brothers, 1962.

Knowles, Malcolm, and Knowles, Hulda. *Introduction to Group Dynamics.* New York: Association Press, 1959.

Kolb, J. H., and Brunner, Edmund deS. *A Study of Rural Society.* Reprint of 1952 ed. Westport, Conn.: Greenwood Press, 1971.

Lee, Robert, ed. *The Church and the Exploding Metropolis.* Richmond: John Knox Press, 1965.

Leiffer, Murray H. *Changing Expectations and Ethics in the Professional Ministry.* Evanston, Ill.: Bureau of social and Religious Research. (Garrett Theological seminary), 1969.

———. *The Effective City Church.* Nashville: Abingdon Press, 1961 (o.p.).

Lindgren, Alvin L. *Foundations for Purposeful Church Administration.* Nashville: Abingdon Press, 1965.

Mills, Harlow S. *The Making of a Country Parish.* New York: Missionary Education Movement in the United States and Canada, 1914 (o. p.).

Minar, David W., and Greer, Scott, eds. *The Concept of Community: Readings with Interpretations.* Chicago: Aldine Publishing Co., 1969.

McElvaney, William K. *The Saving Possibility.* Nashville: Abingdon Press, 1971.

Nelson, Lowry; Ramsey, Charles E.; and Verner, Cooley. *Community Structure and Change.* New York: The Macmillan Co., 1960 (o. p.).

Nelson, Lowry. *Rural Sociology: Its Origin and Growth in the United States.* Minneapolis: University of Minnesota Press, 1969.

Nisbet, Robert A. *Quest for Community.* New York: Oxford University Press, 1962.

Queen, Stuart A., and Carpenter, David B. *The American City.* Reprint of 1953 ed. Westport, Conn.: Greenwood Press, 1971.

Reitz, Rüdiger. *The Church in Experiment.* Nashville: Abingdon Press, 1969.

Rogers, Everett M. *Social Change in Rural Society.* New York: Appleton-Century-Crofts, 1960.

Ross, Murray G., Lappin, B. W. *Community Organization: Theory and Principles.* 2nd ed. New York: Harper & Row, 1967.

Sanders, Irwin T. *The Community: An Introduction to a Social System.* 2nd ed. New York: Ronald Press, 1966.

———. *Making Good Communities Better.* rev. ed. Lexington: University of Kentucky Press, 1953.

Sanderson, Ross W. *The Church Serves the Changing City.* New York: Harper & Brothers, 1955.

Schaller, Lyle E. *The Change Agent.* Nashville: Abingdon Press, 1972.

———. *Parish Planning.* Nashville: Abingdon Press, 1971.

———. *Planning for Protestantism in Urban America.* Nashville: Abingdon Press, 1965.

Shippey, Frederick A. *Church Work in the City.* Nashville: Abingdon Press, 1952 (o. p.).

Sills, Horace S., ed. *Grassroots Ecumenicity: Case Studies in Local Church Consolidation.* Philadelphia: United Church Press, 1967 (o.p.).

Smith, Arthur C. *Team and Group Ministry.* Westminster, England: Church Information Office, 1965.

Smith, Rockwell C. *Rural Ministry and the Changing Community.* Nashville: Abingdon Press, 1971.

Spiegel, Hans B. C., and Mittenthal, Stephen D., *Neighborhood Power and Control: Implications for Urban Planning.* New York:

Institute of Urban Environment, Columbia University School of Architecture, 1968.

Stotts, Herbert E. *The Church Inventory Handbook.* Denver: Wesley Press, 1951.

Taylor, Lee, and Jones, Arthur R., Jr. *Rural Life and Urbanized Society.* New York: Oxford University Press, 1964.

Terry, George R. *Principles of Management.* 5th ed. Homewood, Ill.: Richard D. Irwin, 1968.

Tönnies, Ferdinand. *Community and Society.* Translated and edited by Charles P. Loomis. New York: Harper Torchbooks, 1963.

Vidich, Arthur J.; Bensman, Joseph; and Stein, Maurice R. *Reflections on Community Studies.* New York: Harper Torchbooks, 1971.

Warren, Roland L. *The Community in America.* Chicago: Rand McNally & Company, 1963.

Warren, Rolland. *Truth, Love and Social Change.* Chicago: Rand McNally & Company, 1971.

Webber, George W. *The Congregation in Mission.* Nashville: Abingdon Press, 1964.

———. *God's Colony in Man's World.* Nashville: Abingdon Press, 1960.

Wilson, Robert L., and Davis, James H. *The Church in the Racially Changing Community.* Nashville: Abingdon Press, 1966.

Index